DIGITAL BODY LANGUAGE

By Steven Woods

New Year Publishing LLC
Danville, California

DIGITAL BODY LANGUAGE

by Steven Woods

Published by:
New Year Publishing LLC
144 Diablo Ranch Ct.
Danville, CA 94506 USA

orders@newyearpublishing.com
http://www.newyearpublishing.com

ISBN: 978-0-9799885-5-4

CONTENTS

ACKNOWLEDGEMENTS

A project such as the writing of a book cannot be done without the help of numerous people in a multitude of ways. This book was no exception, and I would not have been able to complete it without the assistance of so many people along the way. To each of you who helped out, with ideas, encouragement, assistance, enthusiasm, or stories, thank you. I could not have done it without you.

First, to the team who made all the details of writing and publishing a book possible, thank you for the efforts you each put into this book. To Dave Morris and the team at New Year Publishing, a big thanks for keeping everything moving along smoothly, and juggling all the parts that make up a book. To Mike Dowding, a heartfelt thanks for continued revisions of the copy and pushing hard for some tight deadlines. To Val Sherer, thanks for your continued patience with our many last minute changes, alterations, and tweaks. To Wendy Fisher and team at Digital Brewing, thanks for some great work, and great designs for cover art.

And to the clients who not only made the stories in this book possible, but who also have made Eloqua such an enjoyable experience over the past decade, thank you for continuing to push the limits in marketing. Teresa Almaraz, Ian Brown, Peter Charleton, Hollis Chin, Drew Clarke, Mark DiMaurizio, Patty Foley-Reid, Greg Forrest, Dean Harrison, Jeff Hartley, Steve Heibein, Gregg

Holzrichter, Amede Hungerford, Dave Laberge, Matisha Ladiwala, Helena Lewis, Amandah Magnarelli, Heather Margolis, Amy Marks, Terry Meehan, Jessica Palmer, Michele Perry, Karin Pindle, Mital Poddar, Will Pringle, Amy Randers, Paul Rosien, Kris Slethaug, Denise Sparks, Heather Stokes, Jordan Weiss, and Jeff Yee, thanks for some great conversations and inspiring case studies.

For the Eloqua team, so many of you helped out in one way or another it is difficult to call out any names in particular. Thank you to each of you who contributed stories, built out ideas, reviewed content, or helped with logistics. Jocelyn, Chad, Anita, Adrian, Ed, Andrew, Chris, Mike, and Nadia, thanks for your help with the stories and case studies that bring life to the book. Steve G., thanks for all your help with the logistics and keeping everything moving along. Joe, thanks for encouraging and supporting the idea of a book as it got off the ground. Jen, Jim, Claudia, thanks for reviewing, challenging, and contributing so many of the ideas in this book. Mercedes, thank you for your continued help with all the legal aspects of the book. Abe, Andrea, Paul, Ralf, Stu, Greg, thanks for sticking with it since the very early days in order to build a great company. And to the rest of the team, thank you for everything you continue to do to build, sell, and deliver the software that makes our clients leaders in their field, and makes this book possible.

Lastly, and most importantly, thank you to my wife Amita, my parents, and my family, for ongoing encouragement, support, and inspiration throughout the entire process.

INTRODUCTION

The whirlwind of change that has been happening in marketing over the past decade could be seen as chaotic, unstructured, and unpredictable. In many ways, those adjectives are very applicable. Underlying it all though, are a few simple changes in how buyers obtain information, and how the ways in which that information is requested and absorbed can provide marketers with unprecedented insights. With those insights, not only can marketers better assist in nurturing prospective buyers, and engaging sales with only those who are ready to purchase, but more importantly can provide strategic insights into optimizing the entire process for growing revenue.

Over the past 9 years at Eloqua, we have had the pleasure of working with many of the world's best marketers in a variety of industries that share a common trait – a significant amount of information is exchanged between buyer and seller throughout the buying process. Whether in Business to Business buying processes, or high value Business to Consumer buying processes, this need to exchange information, combined with the many ways of exchanging it that the Internet continues to provide, has led to a fundamental rethinking of the role of marketing in many organizations.

As we worked with these marketers throughout the world, we noticed a few trends coming to light. The first was a movement towards using marketing to find insights into prospect interests. Information that was provided was done so with an eye towards gaining a better understanding of where in their buying cycle the prospect was. Each insight into the prospective buyer's area and level of interest provided a tiny part of an overall picture of the buyer. By piecing these insights together into a complete picture, the best marketers were able to craft a new way of thinking about marketing. Rather than a campaign-centered, introspective view of their world, they were taking a buyer-centered view of the world. Each message, its targeting, its timing, its content, was thought about in terms of who the buyer was and where in their buying cycle they might be.

This trend led to the second major trend we saw while working with the best marketers. Marketing was re-establishing itself as strategically relevant to the business. For the first time, marketing was able to provide detailed, metric-backed insights into buyers and their goals. Similarly, marketing was able to commit to precise metrics on qualified leads, pipeline contribution, and influenced revenue. By doing so, not only was the alignment between sales and marketing greatly improved, but also the alignment between marketing and the rest of the business.

Marketers who are succeeding in today's environment have understood one key thing. When information is exchanged with a prospective buyer, the insights one can gain by understanding who consumed the information, and why, are as important as the information itself. Much like the experienced salesperson who understands just the right message for each person and knows when to push for the sale and when not to, all through reading the room and observing body language, today's best marketers understand how to read their buyers' digital body language. Through reading that digital body language, these top marketers know when and what to communicate, and know when to bring a salesperson into a deal and when not to. Through reading that digital body language, today's best marketers have gained unprecedented insight into how best to grow their businesses.

This book combines the stories of many of today's best marketers with a narrative that explores the trends that guide the overall evolution of marketing. Overall, the book provides a way of thinking about marketing distilled from years of working on challenging marketing problems with some of the best practitioners in the field. Being a marketer, however, is a journey, and one that is never finished. Many of the concepts presented in this book are concepts that can, and should, be refined continually over time. For that reason, there are many tips included to enable you to get started now. The sooner you start, the sooner you begin to understand how best to refine these concepts to fit your business.

x

ONE

A Transformed
Buying Process

With the advent of many new technologies, there are often two distinct phases to their impact on the way things are done. First, the technology is adopted, but it is used in a similar manner to the prior solution, although often with significant incremental improvements. Then, as a second wave of change, the new capabilities are thought about in entirely novel ways, and the original problem is framed in a fundamentally different manner, leading to sweeping innovations in business practice.

As examples of this phenomenon, we can look at a few technology changes that have shaped the last few decades. Typewriters were replaced with word processors, printed encyclopedia sets were replaced with CD ROM versions, paper maps were replaced with online mapping software. In each of these examples, the initial technology transition added significant value. However, it was the second phase of the transition that ultimately had the broadest impact.

Rather than just easier editing and spell checking, the move of documents to digital format fundamentally changed the way we collaborate and share information. Beyond just richer media and a more portable format, the transition of encyclopedias to digital format caused us as a society to rethink the way we create and share knowledge, and led to innovations such as Wikipedia. The move of maps from paper to digital format enabled a major shift in the way we think about location and interact with maps of the world around us through our cars and cell phones.

Marketing is currently in the middle of a similar shift in thinking. Over the past decade, marketers have seen a tremendous shift in the media types with which they communicate with prospects. Search, email, web, blogs, and video have become common place in marketing campaigns, often more common than television and print. This shift, in itself, has led to many improvements in marketing.

However, the fundamental shift in how marketers think about their role in communicating with prospects is just beginning. As prospective buyers use these online resources to gather the information they require to educate themselves, explore ideas, discover solutions, and form opinions, they do so without any interaction from sales professionals.

The change in how information is gathered is leading to a fundamental change in the nature of marketing and the nature of marketing's relationship with sales. This revolutionary change is even more pronounced and far-reaching when marketing goods and services that are not commodities. In fact, it is a transition that promises to be the dominant force in the reinvention of marketing over the next decade. Marketers who recognize this shifting paradigm and realign their posture to reflect this new reality will regain the strategic relevance that has been threatened in recent years.

THE CONSULTATIVE SALE

Some products and services, of course, elude easy speci-
fication. They are neither simple to understand nor ge-
nerically available. Instead of books or music, the buyer
might be seeking to purchase enterprise software, wealth
management services, corporate insurance, or even
season tickets to a sports event. Typically, the complex
sales process carries a high price tag, reflecting both the
sophistication of the product/service (whether it's a tangible asset or intellectual property of a unique/special-
ized service) as well as the more involved sales process
associated with identifying customers and explaining the
product/service's value.

For instance, the uniqueness of a product or service
means that many buyers may not even be aware they
have the problem that it solves. They may not believe the
pain is solvable. And, of course, they may not be aware
of the vendor's solution. In such a scenario, it might be
tempting for marketers to think that the Internet has
no significant impact on the consultative sale. But is
there really no risk to that process? Can greater access to
information compete with the value that a trained sales
professional brings to a complex sale for highly customized products and services? Some skepticism is probably
in order.

THE SALES PROFESSIONAL

Using a lifetime of relationships and business/social networks to make important contacts and stay abreast of key vertical markets, the consultative sales process is where the sales professional thrives by engaging prospects in trusted conversations and guiding the buyer's thinking on relevant aspects of the buying decision.

It starts with buyer education. Typically, buyers don't enter a complex sales process with the right (or enough) information to understand the scope of the decision. The salesperson must first take the time to understand the buyer's pain points and challenges, painting them in the light of the solution he or she offers.

Through conversations and consultations, the salesperson can educate, guide, and lead a prospective customer through a variety of phases. He uses collateral materials, studies, research, case studies, white papers, anecdotes, references, and events, to ensure the buyer is aware of the pain point and that a viable solution exists and that it can alleviate the pain.

Once convinced that both a pain and solution exist, the buyer starts to evaluate various alternatives. Naturally, there may be a variety of vendors offering competing (though non-identical) solutions, and the buyer begins to weed through the offerings and make comparisons of capabilities. The professional salesperson plays an instrumental role in this process—and pivots from consultant to advisor to seller, positioning his offerings in a way that highlights their ability to solve the prospect's needs. Assuming that the salesperson successfully emerges from this evaluation as the preferred choice of the buyer, he negotiates and closes a contract with the buyer who executes the purchase transaction.

Throughout this process—which can span many months for big-ticket items—the sales professional plays an indispensable role. At every step, he provides the buyer with the right information and the right messages in the right format at the right time. Without someone playing that role as trusted advisor, the buyer may fail to see the seller's advantages and fall sway to another seller's competing solution—or no solution at all.

READING BODY LANGUAGE

A true sales professional develops an innate ability to "read" the nuances of the buyer—an ability that often separates the top performers from the pack of "order-takers." Who is digging in their heels? Who is a motivated buyer? Who is interested in the product? Who is the ultimate economic buyer and what does he need to be convinced?

The ability to "read the room" and identify the right influencers and coaches depends on the ability to identify and interpret body language—non-verbal communication such as crossed arms, head-nodding, a raised eyebrow, shared glances, and other dynamics. Even the most trivial gesture can reveal critical information that a sales professional can use to his advantage.

Understanding the body language enables the salesperson to understand what message is appropriate—right there and then—and adjust on the fly. A buyer squinting in disbelief with a tilted head is asking for more proof points. A buyer who is reluctant to make eye contact may be worried that a new solution can have a negative personal impact and harbors objections that the salesperson must uncover and overcome. A buyer who is nodding his head is someone who wants to accelerate the presentation—and who may be a valuable coach in identifying other internal advocates.

THE INTERNET AND THE COMPLEX SALE: NEW DYNAMICS

Today, this classic model is changing. With the advent of the Internet, the behavior of buyers—the way they identify, understand, evaluate, and buy products—has fundamentally changed.

MARKET EDUCATION AND AWARENESS

The markets in which today's executives operate are dynamic and competitive. Buyers must remain vigilant to stay abreast of fast-changing developments in their industries, ranging from shifting regulatory environments to trends in consumer behavior. Globalization creates

⇨ GET STARTED NOW

BE FINDABLE

Before you even get outbound campaigns underway, before you rent lists, before you start writing clever copy—think about the buyer's first step. Think about where future buyers go to educate themselves, discover solutions, or make comparisons. That's where you want to be. And that means making sure you're easily findable and prominent on major search engines using the key phrases that are likely to be in buyers' minds.

---

new markets—and new competitors. New supply chains and ecosystems of partners, suppliers, and distributors shift constantly, and, of course, technological advances can quickly rewrite the rules for capabilities, costs, and timeframes.

It's a daunting challenge for buyers who have quickly embraced the power of the Internet to aggregate diverse and valuable resources. Industry Web sites and e-newsletters (most of which are free of charge), for example, offer detailed and up-to-date information on trends and developments in concise and convenient formats. Vendors, too, are stepping up to the plate with their own specific Web sites, focused micro-sites, downloadable information, views from selected industry analysts, and other resources that reinforce their views of the important trends.

FINDING POSSIBLE SOLUTIONS

As all of these resources and capabilities become increasingly ubiquitous, buyers must ensure these trends and information align with their business needs in order to narrow their explorations. After all, resources and expertise are perennially in short supply—addressing the appropriate business pain in the right manner is key.

Hand-in-hand, globalization and the Internet are also dismantling some of the traditional constraints of geography and time—software can be downloaded, hardware can be ordered and express-shipped, services can be outsourced offshore, and consultants can be flown in. Today's markets for sophisticated solutions are reaching a level of global availability that is, in many respects, breathtaking to contemplate.

The Internet—and especially Web 2.0 technologies—have emerged to facilitate this important process. Podcasts and on-demand webinars, for example, bring a variety of information to busy buyers. Blogs, in particular, are connecting buyer communities across the world and enabling a level of information sharing and product comparison that was unthinkable even a few years ago. Colleagues and peers can share their insights and experiences in detail—without the mediation of a vendor.

The rise of search giants has also fundamentally reformed the process of discovering solutions and potential vendor options. A quick search of Google or Yahoo!

yields a very useful list of vendor options and resources of varying depth and perspectives.

Of course, vendors also play a role here as well, offering tools for detecting and analyzing the existence and scope of a business pain as well as assessing the potential economic impact associated with various steps to address the pain. Ensuring the right options have been considered is critical to selecting the right solution.

NEW SOURCES OF VALIDATION

Buying a complex product or service is a particularly challenging process of sorting through a range of competing claims and promises from vendors of varying credibility and trustworthiness. Will there be cost overruns? Will schedules slip? Is there a pattern of missed expectations? Buyers historically have been in the dark—often relying on the references and assurances of the vendor's hand-picked customers. This is not to say that vendor malfeasance is the reason (although it certainly can be one cause). An improper selection can often be related to mismatched objectives and capabilities—a mismatch that can be difficult to identify early in the process of validating a solution. Given the investments typically involved, that's a risky proposition that can have disastrous implications if things go wrong.

Perhaps more than any other phase of the complex sale, this validation aspect has felt the most profound impact.

A basic download of a solution can provide prompt and simple validation while community sites can show the good and bad of the entire customer experience for potential buyers to review. Interactive videos and images provide detailed presentations, models, and simulations of products, helping the buyer see a clearer picture of the proposed solution.

THE VANISHING SALES REP?

The sources of information available to buyers of complex products—that have traditionally required a consultative sales process—continue to grow in volume and quality. In the past decade, a buyer has achieved new capabilities to understand an industry's trends, translate that into business pain/opportunity that can be addressed, assemble a list of potential vendors, and analyze the best solution for their specific needs. The point to note: not one of these new sources has required the involvement of a sales professional.

Buyers are leveraging these new information sources, rendering the salesperson to a secondary role (or even a non-presence)—particularly early in the process. As the professional salesperson somewhat fades from view, so, too, does his ability to observe and understand the buyer. Because of his absence, he cannot read the room by carefully watching the buyer's body language. He is unaware who holds the purse, who has the objections, and who is an advocate.

This lack of awareness puts him in a very precarious position—unable to effectively guide the sales process. Advocates can't be cultivated. Decision-makers can't be identified. Blockers can't be discovered and pre-emptively handled. Without these key insights and responsive strategies, the sales professional is blind to the true motivations and agendas of the buyer participants—and significantly hamstrung in his ability to shape and influence the purchase process.

TIMING IS EVERYTHING?

In this environment, it is far more challenging to align the prospect's *buying process* with the company's *selling process*—which are no longer synonymous. And that carries significant implications for lead qualification and hand-off. When a prospect appears on the corporate Web site—perhaps to download a white paper—he is most likely merely "kicking the tires" and is not ready to buy. As a result, the sales rep disqualifies the lead and ejects the prospect from the funnel. It's not that the prospect isn't going to buy—he's just not going to buy right now.

This creates the "leaky funnel" with which most marketers are painfully familiar. They devote huge efforts to generating raw leads, but if those leads aren't in a perfectly synchronized phase of their buying process, the sales team will waste marketing's efforts by ignoring the lead. Sirius Decisions found that, of the leads passed over to sales, only a shockingly low 20 percent actually received follow-up from the rep. Of that 20 percent, the rep sets aside 70 percent of them as "disqualified"— even though subsequent objective analysis shows that 80 percent of them eventually buy a solution (usually from another company). They were good leads—just early leads.

As this transition happens, marketers who understand, guide, and facilitate the buying process are able to have a real and measurable impact on both revenue and sales effectiveness. By ensuring that the message for each potential buyer maps to their interests and stage in the buying process, more inquiries can be generated. By focusing on passing leads to sales that are in an active buying stage, rather than tire kicking, the number of leads qualified by sales will increase, even as raw numbers of leads passed decreases.

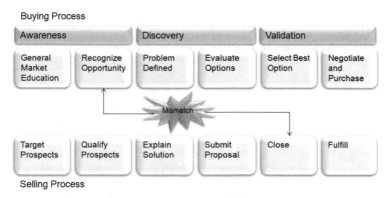

Figure 1: The mismatch between buying and selling processes often leads to salespeople attempting to close deals with prospects that are early in their buying process, leading to funnel leakage.

THE IMPLICATIONS FOR MARKETING

Historically, marketers in organizations using a consultative sales process have had somewhat more limited roles than in, say, CPG industries. In these companies, the direct sales force in the field has been the center of power while marketing has focused on generating awareness and brand management. Marketing provides a tactical level of support through collateral, case studies, demand management, and events.

However, as the dynamics among buyers continue to shift –with new and trusted sources of information enabling buyers to self-educate—the role of the marketer must also shift. Today's marketers are keenly aware of these new information sources and extra-company conversations, of course. The overriding question is: what should they do about it? What are the new communications vehicles—and which ones are right for the organization's industry and market? What marketing-infrastructure investments make the most sense? What is the right media mix?

Unless marketers fundamentally alter their thinking about marketing and forego traditional approaches, they will completely miss the tectonic shifts that are taking place in buyers' worlds. Online marketing is more than search-engine optimization. A video blog isn't like a TV channel. A downloadable trial version of software is not merely a free sample—any more than a computer is a paperless typewriter. Such perceptions miss the fundamentally revolutionary nature of the changes.

The complex, consultative process is experiencing dramatic shifts that are transforming the very way in which buyers conduct transactions as they accrue and exercise new power. Marketers who adapt to this new buying reality will thrive. Those who don't will find themselves consigned to a steady erosion of relevance, influence, and value.

TWO

THE BUYER'S NEW
TOOL KIT

As today's buyers embrace a new suite of information resources, today's marketers must make the effort to truly understand these sources and how buyers are using them to self-educate and form opinions about their products and services. Such an analysis is a prerequisite for making reasonable decisions about investments in new media and marketing channels.

The complexity of a product or service is typically matched with an equally complex sales process that emphasizes education and consultation. Most talented sales professionals intimately understand the complexity of the sales process once the prospective buyer has initiated the process and engaged with the vendor organization. But, increasingly, a tremendous amount of education and research is preceding this step—and this pre-vendor phase is a far less structured proposition. The sales professional is likely unaware the process is underway and that the buyer is already forming opinions and assessing options.

Buyers typically proceed through a three-phase education process in the early stages of the procurement cycle. While these phases aren't as discrete as presented below, this framework helps us better understand matters from the buyer's perspective.

⇨ *GET STARTED NOW*

SHOW—DON'T TELL

Whether it's general background or specific details, buyers want information—not marketing spiels. That's especially true at the early stages of the buying cycle. Re-orient your marketing thinking to guide prospects through their education and discovery process by understanding and presenting the exact information they need at each step

PHASE 1: SOLUTION AWARENESS AND MARKET EDUCATION

In this first phase, the buyer has an acquisitive mind-set, seeking as much relevant information as possible. Business executives continually seek out, sift through, explore, and exchange ideas about their market or sector—a continuous process that is integrated into their daily lives as part of their larger mission and responsibility. The scope of topics can be quite broad—from regulatory changes to the macroeconomic environment—and the goal is to gain as clear of a multi-year picture as possible. Part of this constant survey can include seeking out new techniques for production, learning about technologies that improve productivity, identifying market opportunities, and optimizing current opportunities.

For example, case studies of competitors or comparative industry peers enable them to benchmark their efforts

⇨ *GET STARTED NOW*

KNOW WHEN TO ASK FOR INFORMATION

As you re-orient your marketing to show not tell, make sure you start to fully understand your prospects at each stage. As they require information, it's OK to ask for an equitable amount of reciprocating information in return. For a five-minute online demo, you could ask for basic contact information. For a one-hour webinar, it's entirely legitimate to request more information on their buying process. At each step, leverage the information you already have so that you're asking only a minimal set of incremental questions.

---

and results. Interviews with industry analysts, industry newsletters, blogs, trade journal archives, and conference papers are some of the popular tools and sources in this phase. Discussions of the concepts and techniques from other industries can also provide excellent inspiration for innovative approaches in their own industry.

Over time, the buyer encounters concepts that speak to a recognizable pain that exists and that resonates with and adds value to her organization. Either through events internal to her organization, or through understanding the concept in a new level of depth that increases its urgency, the pain moves to near the top of the corporate agenda. From there, the buyer moves to discover what solutions may exist to address that pain.

PHASE 2: SOLUTION DISCOVERY

When the buyer transitions to this stage, he has a specific business pain in mind and is exploring the market to gain a sense of what solution might be able to meet that challenge. This transition from awareness and education to solution discovery is often precipitated by a compelling business event, such as a high-visibility incident, corporate restructuring, merger, or acquisition. Such an event often brings sometimes-latent business pain to the surface. Regardless, it becomes a catalyst, creates a greater sense of urgency, and narrows the research to specific solutions that address the identified pain point.

The prospective buyer is trying to understand the complete range of potential solutions. Who are the relevant vendors in this space? What are the high-level specifics about those solutions—for instance, is it an outsourced solution, a piece of technology, or a consulting engagement? What information is available to help investigate the offering further? What is the "ballpark impact" of the proposed solution on the budget?

PHASE 3. SOLUTION VALIDATION

Once a prospect learns enough to understand the business pain and assemble a prioritized list of vendors offering potentially relevant solutions, he begins to delve into the alternatives more deeply to start the critical process of determining which choice is the best fit for his organization. In many procurement cycles, this

---

▷ *GET STARTED NOW*

WHEN NEEDED, EDUCATE THE MARKET

Is your target market looking for your type of solution directly—or only for the general category you fit into? Sometimes you need to educate prospects to help them understand the pain you solve. Work toward that goal by providing thought leadership. Regularly review search-term frequency reports to understand how buyers educate themselves on your general market and specific category.

---

milestone is accompanied by the formation of a broader (often multi-disciplinary) team to investigate and analyze the proposed solution from a variety of important aspects: department and technological interactions, personnel questions, purchasing economics, and more. The buyer typically has many questions:

- What are the capabilities?

- How will my team deploy it?

- What services will I need?

- How much will it cost now and in the future? What is the total cost of ownership (TCO)?

- What skills will my organization need?

- How does it interact with and affect my current business processes?

The questions that buyers ask will depend, of course, on the solution under consideration. Finance may have very different questions regarding a consulting engagement compared to an IT group's questions regarding hardware procurement. Nonetheless, the goal is the same. The prospective buyer wants to know what is being offered for sale, what the price is, whether it solves the identified business pain, and what the impact will be on the organization.

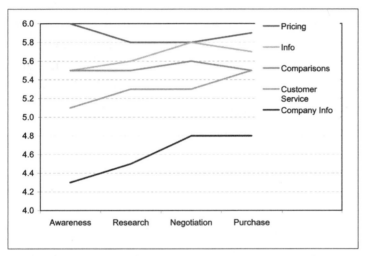

Figure 2: Marketing Sherpa shows the evolution of buyers' information needs as they move through a buying process

THE COMPONENTS OF THE TOOLKIT

Traditionally, this education process has been guided by the trained, knowledgeable sales professional who understands what's involved at each milestone and what the buyer needs to know. His ability to read the buyer's body language enables him to guide the process based on each participant's demonstrated levels of interest and engagement. Today, of course, that opportunity is largely disappearing because the sales professional doesn't enter the picture until much later—after the education and solution discovery are complete (or nearly so).

Most tools that educate prospective buyers are relevant to more than one aspect of the buying process—so this simplification to three phases inevitably loses the nuances and complexities that any process has. However, it allows us to cut through much of the noise surrounding technology and information sources on the market today and concentrate on what matters: ensuring the right person receives the right message in the right format at the right time. The following list is not exhaustive. However, it is a useful categorization of several of the more popular tools and sources that shape this book's framework.

Industry News Sites and Newsletters

Like their hard-copy counterparts, industry Web sites and newsletters present specialized industry information, emerging trends to consider, best practices (proven and proposed), and ideas. These sites generally strive to deliver content that is free from vendor bias—and they achieve that to varying degrees. Although there is certainly some inevitable bias stemming from the economic realities of advertising, industry sites and newsletters do an admirable job of providing objective information on the relevant trends and changes that affect the industry. Many newer sites supplement industry news with insightful analysis and commentary on vendors and their

⇨ *GET STARTED NOW*

VIRAL: SET YOUR MESSAGE FREE

The runaway success of a few well-known viral campaigns masks the shortcomings of the great majority of messages that quickly faded into oblivion. Done well, viral marketing can be a tremendously cost-effective technique for generating awareness. The key is separation: make sure the part of the message that makes it viral-worthy (the funny, irreverent, "can-you-believe-it" component) should be quite distinct from your brand or awareness message. If they're tied too tightly together, you end up with a "commercial" message that does not spread.

---

respective offerings. In this manner, these sites act more as industry analysts—which increases their value to and credibility with buyers.

From the buyer's perspective, the industry sites' main impact is during the awareness phase. Executives and prospective buyers can browse industry sites to remain current with their industry. Through that education, they become aware of, and more familiar with, many new potential categories of solutions. This is an important service to the buyer.

INDUSTRY ANALYSTS

Industry analysts are seasoned experts who provide well-informed, objective commentary on the vendors providing solutions relevant to a particular industry. These analyses give buyers insightful views into specific solutions, how those solutions compare with one another, what the important decision metrics are, and the strengths and weaknesses of vendors relative to those metrics. Typically, this commentary is delivered across a variety of media types: published research studies, white papers, conferences, events, and webinars to name just a few.

This industry analysis becomes a very useful starting point for buyers who leverage the analyst's perspective to gain a better understanding of the vendors in a space, or in framing their evaluation of vendors.

	Awareness	Discovery	Validation
Industry News	☆☆☆	☆	☆
Industry Analysts	☆☆	☆☆	☆☆☆
Advertising	☆☆	☆☆☆	
Viral Messages	☆☆☆	☆☆	
Podcasts	☆	☆	☆☆☆
Search	☆	☆☆☆	☆☆
Webinars	☆☆☆	☆	☆☆
Tradeshows	☆☆	☆☆☆	☆
Blogs	☆☆☆	☆	☆☆
Vendor Sites	☆☆	☆☆☆	☆☆

Figure 3: Use of different marketing vehicles by buyers at stages of the buying process.

ADVERTISING

Internet advertising enables the marketer to deliver a brief, targeted message to a qualified, narrowly defined audience in a far more targeted manner than television or radio could ever achieve. Admittedly, even Internet advertising's level of precision can be improved upon—it still paints the market with a very broad brush, using only broad demographics such as job title, role/responsibility, or industry.

Nonetheless, advertising can sometimes be a very effective component of the marketing mix in a complex sales process by ensuring that an audience is aware of a vendor as an option to solve a particular business challenge. If a skilled marketer can distill a complex solution to a memorable message that can be consumed at a glance, advertising can even facilitate buyers' awareness that a solution category exists.

VIRAL MESSAGES

Consumer media offer numerous marketing platforms that are generally ignored by most business-to-business marketers. This is, in many instances, a grave oversight. Facebook, MySpace, Twitter, YouTube, and many similar platforms provide interesting new ways to market that B2B marketers would be wise to consider. As B2B marketers find ways to adapt these media and channels into their marketing mixes, we will see some of these media evolve from exotic choices to mainstream staples. Many

KADIENT: BLOGGING ABOUT INTERNAL PROCESSES CONNECTS WITH BUYERS

Kadient's move into Software as a Service (SaaS) brought with it a fundamental shift in their marketing to connect more deeply with their buyer and user audience. A company-wide effort to develop and use buyer and user personas sparked numerous discussions on exactly how "Luke" or "Anya", and several other personas, would use the product in his or her daily life, and how it should be built, marketed, and sold in order to best connect with him or her.

As they focused more on connecting with their buyers, Kadient fleshed out the personalities with increasing detail. Hobbies, personality traits, and even cardboard cutouts were created to provide insights into Anya and Luke. When a development or marketing meeting was held to discuss the market, the discussion would always focus around their buyer and user personas.

This effort was then noticed by David Meerman Scott, an influential industry blogger and writer, who highlighted Kadient's efforts in his online forum. Although the main topic of the writing was the use of buyer and user personas, Kadient was identified as a leader in their field. Anya and Luke were highlighted in detail, allowing any reader of the blog to identify with their goals and challenges.

Two other industry bloggers, Charles Brown and Scott Sehlhorst of Tyner Blain, quickly picked up the story, and added their own commentary, further establishing Kadient as a company intently focused on the success of their customers. A Google blog search for Kadient shows these blogs highlighted at the top of the results, adding credibility to any buyer considering Kadient's solutions. The combined traffic of these blogs was estimated at more than 20,000 regular viewers.

A 37% spike in web traffic to the Kadient site corresponding to this discussion on the blogs highlighted to the Kadient marketing team the importance to their prospective buyers of a company dedicated to continual understanding of the buyers' needs. Although this was not an effort that generated direct sales leads, the value it provided in awareness and credibility was tremendous, and the cost was essentially zero.

of these platforms provide opportunities for exposure and awareness that would be difficult to achieve in other media.

Viral marketing is one such example of an opportunity in these new media. Innovative business-to-business marketers, have been experimenting with viral marketing techniques in their marketing efforts in an effort to leverage the social, lighthearted, and entertaining aspects of new media to gain exposure to a more business oriented message.

Viral marketing uses messages with two distinct aspects. The first component is compelling content. The message must be interesting, enticing, or entertaining enough to entice a recipient to forward it to a friend or colleague. The second component is a message that is carefully crafted to contain positioning and messaging that the marketer wants to share and spread among his target market/constituency.

Generally, the marketing message is a small part of the overall campaign, with much of the emphasis on entertainment to encourage forwarding in linear or geometric progressions. Successful viral campaigns can drive strong awareness, but rarely deliver the more detailed and nuanced positioning required for solution validation.

It's quite likely that viral marketing will continue to see a steady evolution from historically consumer-oriented media types toward the B2B realm as marketers adapt it to their unique requirements. Many of these campaigns will, by their nature, contribute to the awareness phase. However, each media type has its own properties and should be evaluated on its own merits and strengths.

Podcasts

The iPod ushered in an innovative reapplication of an old medium—audio. Today, there is a thriving "podcast market" where company executives and industry luminaries record and publish brief segments that listeners can subscribe to and consume (often while commuting or traveling). Executives can stay abreast of trends in their industry by listening in on the rough equivalent of a highly targeted, industry-specific radio show.

This is a lower-cost medium that marketers have found most beneficial in establishing thought-leadership positions within their industries. By providing educational content, interviews, and discussions, marketers can maintain an active and interested listenership while

CONCUR: AWARENESS AND DISCOVERY THROUGH VIRAL STORIES

Concur, a leader in travel and expense management, wanted to engage more with the end-user of their service, a business traveler, who could act as a champion within an organization that might purchase Concur's service. To do so, they wanted to use viral marketing to increase both awareness of its solutions for travel-expense management and the level of engagement they had with this audience. The concept: travel nightmares. After all, every business traveler has his or her stories of lost luggage, hotel disasters, and chance encounters with odd characters.

Concur tapped into these shared miseries and entertaining stories by creating a Web 2.0 site that enabled visitors to submit their own brief travel stories. The site offered mechanisms for visitors to engage with the stories—they could be read, browsed, forwarded to friends, rated, or commented on.

Once a critical mass of content was in place, Concur generated traffic both from the main Concur.com site as well as from print and banner advertisements. Additional traffic was driven virally as travelers shared stories and forwarded the site to their peers.

Throughout the process, the Concur team carefully inserted elements to build awareness of its own solutions for travel expense management and encouraged readers to learn more about products or sign up for Concur® Expense—Trial Edition, a free trial of the company's expense reporting service. Although run as essentially separate campaigns, the free trial campaign provided a great action for prospects to take if they saw an interest in the Concur offering.

broadening their awareness in their target market regarding key trends and developments. A relationship with key industry analysts is a great strategy to increase credibility—particularly in the latter stages of solution validation.

Search

Search-engine marketing and search-engine optimization give marketers a new and interesting media type to leverage. By targeting buyers using their search phrases, marketers can achieve a very attractive level of precision and granularity regarding buyer demographics and interests. What's more, the nature of online search—with its flexibility, control, and cost-effectiveness—often creates an attractive economic proposition.

Most marketing teams focusing on complex products and sales cycles are well aware of the opportunities that search-engine marketing and search-engine optimization present. In fact, many actively use it as a key component of their marketing efforts. However, simply running keyword ads won't have a dramatic impact. It is essential to understand how buyers use search as part of their buying process, to achieve the best possible return on the marketing investment.

Generally, buyers use search in just the manner that the name implies - searching—typically in the discovery phase of the process. Here, a buyer recognizes that he has

NETQOS: VIRAL MARKETING FOR AWARENESS

NetQoS markets to a challenging audience: network engineers running advanced network operations centers (NOCs). It would be a huge understatement to call this skeptical audience "marketing-averse." They generally devote significant efforts to eluding even the best marketing communications of every sort. NetQoS realized that it needed another way to connect with this group.

Realizing this audience was very comfortable with online media such as blogs, gaming, and various social-networking sites, NetQoS crafted a campaign that leveraged these channels to increase awareness of NetQoS in its target market. NetQoS's own lab developed a way to present network data—traffic, packets, server errors, etc.—in a video game motif, complete with 3-D visuals and pyrotechnics.

With a careful seeding strategy in blogs, on Slashdot, Digg, Reddit, Twitter, and Flickr, this YouTube video—"The anatomy of a Slashdot post"—became an immediate success. Within the first 12 hours, it was viewed more than 66,000 times and picked up on more than 70 blogs and a number of mainstream media outlets. NetQoS carefully crafted its embedding of links to its commercial offerings so the viral success led to marketing success as well.

The goal of this campaign was to drive product awareness through the viral video. By creating an easy path from the viral video to product information, NetQoS drove a 400-percent increase in trial downloads during the month of the campaign. Simultaneously, exposure on Google increased by 41 percent across all search terms and more than 600 percent on the search term most related to the viral video.

a business pain that requires a solution and is now working to understand available solutions.

In addition, search also plays a crucial role in the validation phase of the process as buyers attempt to explore various sources of information on the solutions they are validating in order to identify or resolve objections.

WEBINARS

Webinars have become a trusted way for sellers to communicate a complex message to a wide audience of prospective buyers. Either live, or recorded (on-demand), a webinar provides a smart, controlled way to present an industry luminary or vendor expert to discuss topics that are important to buyers.

The audience for most webinars draws from a broad swath of industry participants. These 45-60-minute sessions are often marketed through banner ads (usually on key industry Web sites), shared lists, and opt-in e-mail blasts. Webinars provide a feasible and efficient way to communicate awareness messages to well-defined audiences and start to lay the foundation for solution evaluation. For this reason, most webinars focus on thought-leadership and industry trends.

As the source of this education, an affiliated vendor establishes itself as an important vendor that merits consideration when buyers are seeking a solution. Likewise, the implicit validation through association with an in-

A Marketer's Challenge: Flying Car, Wall Flower, or Red-headed Stepchild

Recasting their marketing in terms of the buying process, marketers must better conceptualize the challenge that they are most focused on in the market. It could be an awareness challenge, a discovery challenge, or a selection challenge. Each requires a slightly different approach.

Challenge	Description	Marketing Focus
Flying Car	A solution that solves a major pain, but most potential buyers do not know that the pain is even solvable, and are therefore not seeking a solution.	Awareness efforts, such as industry newsletters, analyst relations, or even viral campaigns or contests to prove that a solution to the challenge is possible.
Wall Flower	A well-understood category, but potential buyers do not evaluate your solution as part of their investigation efforts.	Solution-discovery efforts such as search, trade-shows, and advertising to ensure that you are invited to compete.
Red-Headed Stepchild	You are invited to compete for business, but often a competitor is selected over your solution.	Validation efforts such as blogs or webinars to establish credibility or influence the decision frameworks of potential buyers.

Use of different marketing vehicles by buyers at stages of the buying process dustry luminary brings added and enhanced credibility to the vendor. This technique creates a solid reputation when the prospective buyer begins to evaluate options.

TRADESHOWS

For many years, this has been a staple for marketers of complex products. Today, the industry tradeshow is still a key component of many marketers' plans. Recently, Internet-based tradeshows have gained prominence as an online corollary to the typical convention center show.

Buyers attend tradeshows for many reasons, but chiefly for the opportunity to efficiently explore available solutions in the industry and quickly engage in a conversation with vendors for those solutions. Tradeshows provide an excellent method for quickly gaining knowledge on trends, vendors, and solutions. Most shows include a full agenda of educational workshops, presentations, speeches, and more, meaning that the tradeshow acts as a significant driver of buyer direction during the awareness and discovery phases of the buying process.

BLOGS

Rising from their roots as essentially online journals, weblogs or blogs have evolved into a media type that is often quite relevant to the marketing of complex products. In most industries, there are a growing number of blogs that are actively maintained and read by industry participants. To the marketer, this presents an interesting opportunity to influence buyers early and influence the sales cycle.

To ensure discovery of the solution, a marketer might participate in (or have a key spokesperson at the company participate in) an industry blog by building a relationship with the blog's author or by contributing in the blog's comments section on topics of relevance. Another alternative is for the marketer to create the company's own blog (under the auspices of the company's spokesperson or designated thought-leader). This creates greater credibility and a higher leadership profile while ensuring a level of control over messaging and positioning.

VENDOR SITES

The vendor Web site remains central to much of the activity the buyer undertakes to gain awareness of industry trends and challenges, learn about potential solutions, and validate the correct solution for their unique situation. The Web site (or any campaign-specific micro-site) acts as an information portal, providing the right information to the prospective buyer at the right time in their buying process—typically during the awareness phase.

The Web site becomes a valuable clearinghouse (one of several) that enables the buyer to educate himself on relevant industry trends. The classic vendor site contains downloadable white papers, thought-leadership articles, and industry studies that are informative. Although much of this education material has an inherent bias and shouldn't be confused with neutral or objective information, the vendor Web site still represents resources that most buyers value by properly recognizing that its source has a commercial objective.

Much of this education occurs outside of the vendor's own Web site, of course. However, successful marketers can often provide pathways to bring in traffic to their Web site and insert themselves into that buyer-education process.

As the buyer prioritizes the relevance and acuity of the business pain and begins to seek solutions, the vendor's Web site provides quickly referenceable information that lets him understand whether the vendor might have an appropriate solution. The more a vendor can influence the awareness phase, the easier it is to ensure its discovery as a viable solution.

During validation, the vendor's Web site becomes a rich source of information, comparisons, trials, and data to assist in the prospective buyer's evaluation. Similarly, marketers can optimally position their solution by leveraging the Web site to steer site visitors to external sources of information that lend validity and credibility to their solution.

THE BUYER'S EVOLUTION

As buyers move away from dependence on a vendor's professional sales team for market education and awareness, solution discovery, and validation, the suite of tools they rely on to source their information continues to evolve in depth and sophistication. Today, marketers must understand the evolution in the buyer's behavior and, more importantly, how to interact with the buyer in this new paradigm to optimally influence the buyer's decisions.

A sales professional's ability to observe and understand the buyer's body language was an irreplaceable component of his success. That's no longer possible in the new paradigm. Instead, marketers must rise to the challenge: marketers must cultivate new skills to observe and understand the buyer's digital body language.

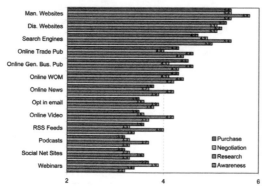

Figure 4: Marketing Sherpa evaluates the relevance of various online sources by stage in the buying process

76ERS:
LIVE INTERACTION AT BUYING POINT OF INTEREST

The sales and marketing team for the Philadelphia 76ers has assets that most marketers can only dream of: a highly recognized brand in their target market and a Web site stocked with exciting content. The challenge: convert that loyalty and excitement into sales of seat packages, season tickets, or luxury suites.

The 76ers recognized they needed to map the selling process to their customers' buying process. Although buying these tickets was definitely a considered purchase, those transactions are also strongly tied to the excitement that the team generates. To leverage that emotional tie, the sales process had to be built around that excitement on the Web site.

Members of the 76ers inside sales team were equipped to respond to live Web chat inquiries from site visitors. Customers could initiate a live Web chat on any critical page that related to ticket purchases. From discount student tickets to corporate suites, the buying process and the selling process were matched up by enabling the buyer and seller to connect over live Web chat.

The results were dramatic. By aligning with the buyer's true, preferred process, the 76ers connected with more potential buyers to answer last-minute questions on seating, playoffs, and game selection. Even the largest deals got a lift from the Web chat as the inside sales team closed an $8,000 corporate suite deal—just by matching up with the customer's buying process.

THREE

WHAT IS DIGITAL BODY LANGUAGE?

As the buyer is progressing through the various phases of the buying process, he interacts with the vendor's organization by seeking, receiving, using, and responding to information. In the past, those interactions were largely face to face or by telephone and the sales professional was able to read the subtle clues and nuances- the forward-leaning posture, the raised eyebrows, the tone of voice, and more.

Can that same level of interaction and interpretation be achieved in the digital world? Can marketers define and read a "digital body language" that offers consistently predictive clues and insights into buyer behavior?

Absolutely.

Digital body language is an art and science that revolves around detecting and understanding prospective buyers' signals and intentions to better communicate with them. The transition that began a decade ago with the arrival of the Internet and its many new sources of information, will require a significant rethinking on the part of marketers, sales professionals, and the organizations they serve.

THE SHIFT IN THE FUNNEL

First and foremost, the increasing relevance of digital body language is creating a very real shift in the hand-off between marketing and sales. Marketing is moving further into the buying process as the buyer leverages new sources of information instead of relationships with sales professionals. That's placing a greater premium on the marketer's ability to create, target, and deliver relevant and credible information.

Similarly, that increasing relevance makes it even more important to capture, understand, and process the subtle signals that are part of the marketing process—even online. In so doing, the marketer can gain an increasing ability to objectively—and more fully—understand the prospective buyer, his purchasing inclinations, intentions, concerns, objections, and more. These breakthrough insights also bring a corresponding responsibil-

---

⇨ *GET STARTED NOW*

TIE E-MAIL TO YOUR WEB SITE

Understanding your prospects' digital body language depends on your ability to decode who visits your Web site. Since e-mail is the most common way to communicate with prospects, ensure your e-mail and Web analytics engines are fully integrated. Each link in every e-mail should provide information to identify the Web site visitor when he clicks through—and throughout all subsequent visits. That will enable your Web analytics solution to identify the visitor.

---

ity to the marketer to ensure that the leads handed off to the sales team reflect those that are most likely to purchase—with appropriate dollar volumes and timeframes.

MARKETING BASED ON DIGITAL BODY LANGUAGE

Once marketers begin to leverage an awareness of the buyer's digital body language, the very approach to marketing itself begins to change. An ever-increasing body of knowledge about where the buyer is in the buying process, what they're interested in, and how interested they are all combine to enable the marketer to target subsequent messaging to the buyer based on that buyer's demonstrated preferences and stage in the buying process.

Traditionally, the best marketers could hope for were campaigns predicated on demographic or firmographic criteria—the target's job title, role, or industry. There was little to no awareness of the stage in the buying process that the prospective buyer was in, leading to messages that did not optimally or fully connect with the intended audience. It's like a sales professional delivering the same presentation to every group of potential buyers while completely disregarding whether they are fully engaged and interested or distant and skeptical. To fully leverage the buyer's digital body language, the marketer must approach marketing process with two important concepts in mind. These two concepts form the foundation of a new approach to thinking about marketing approaches.

1. PROSPECT PROFILING

A marketer must first observe prospects in all interactions with the company. But where can you gather this kind of information on a prospect's area and level of interests? It comes from multiple sources—and, in fact, multiple sources are required to achieve a level of validity.

Like most data analyses, care must be taken in the selection, aggregation, and interpretation. Body language is comprised of multiple tiny details of posture, expression, motion, and tone. But just as we interpret it at a higher level—grouping the signals collectively under the label of "interest" or "hesitation"—so, too, must we interpret digital body language.

2. PROSPECT OR LEAD SCORING

To accurately assess and predict a prospective buyer's buying cycle stage, interest area, or response to a marketing campaign we must aggregate the digital body language into a meaningful—and simple—result that guides how we interact with that individual going forward.

Historical lead-scoring techniques simply leveraged demographic and firmographic information and were used solely for the determination of which leads to pass to sales. Today's marketer leverages a much broader range of a buyer's digital body language to create a lead score with greater validity and accuracy. Now, the marketer can differentiate between a low-value prospective buyer—the ideal title and the right industry but who shows no interest—and a high-value prospective buyer who has an identical title and industry but shows many signs of a very motivated buyer.

Marketers also use the same technique—understanding the prospect's digital body language by applying a score—to guide how the prospect is communicated to, whether they are tuning out of messaging, and whether a campaign has influenced the overall buying decision.

This ability to interpret the buyer's stage and intentions and direct the next steps in the communication process makes digital body language so powerful. The marketer can more clearly and quickly discern which buyers are actively engaged in a buying process and which are not—all based on the clues to buying behavior. By reading these signals and acting accordingly, the marketer can achieve significant successes as they are, for the first time, able to understand and respond to the prospect's buying process.

A FOUNDATION FOR MARKETING

Understanding prospects' digital body language through the two disciplines of prospect profiling and lead (or prospect) scoring form the foundation for today's marketing. On top of this foundation, marketers tackle the four key challenges of marketing to the new buyer.

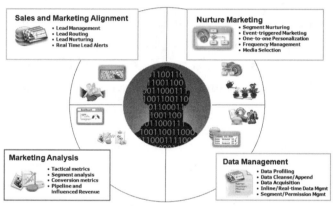

Figure 5: Digital body language forms a core of the four main areas marketers must focus on in a considered-purchase buying process.

CAMPAIGNING—NURTURING IS KEY

The fact is, at any moment, most prospective buyers are not actively engaged in a buying process with you. That's because, as we've seen, a buying process for a complex product or service generally is governed by a combination of factors. First, the prospective buyer must recognize his company has a relevant and meaningful business pain. Next, he must understand the industry/sector well enough to seek a particular solution. And, as discussed, there is often a key internal event that drives action and prioritizes that business pain as the most important one to solve at that moment in time.

Once a marketer profiles the digital body language of the community of potential buyers and translates that into objective scores that define where each buyer is in their buying process, the marketer can then route buyers to the right interaction that makes the most sense for their unique position in the procurement cycle. Buyers showing the proper combination of demographic and firmographic qualifications and the digital body language of an active buyer are immediately passed to sales as hot prospects.

In all likelihood, of course, most prospective clients don't have the right combination of factors in place at the same time and show a digital body language that suggests they are not ready to buy. But that doesn't mean they are unlikely to become actively engaged in a buying process later. It only means that they are not engaged at the current time.

What do you do for these "future likelies"? It's critical to keep them engaged with the right level of communication so that, when their digital body language, objectively scored, changes and indicates that they have moved to a different phase in their buying process, they enter your funnel and progress through the sales cycle. In other words, you need to nurture these leads until they later blossom into a full-fledged prospects.

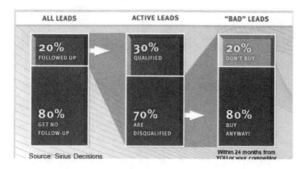

Figure 6: Sirius research shows that, of the 70% of leads who are disqualified by sales, 80% end up buying eventually, often from a competitor.

DATA MANAGEMENT—A NEW DISCIPLINE FOR MARKETING

To capitalize on these insights and opportunities, marketing must not only think about changing the way that messaging is targeted and delivered, it must also develop an entirely new discipline to facilitate the operational, process, and data requirements of digital body language. Marketers who continue to pursue their mission with a disconnected set of communication tools and non-integrated data sets cannot gain the multi-perspective visibility into their prospects that is required to understand and leverage their digital body language. Achieving these new perspectives, however, requires an approach to data, processes, and operations rooted in a new rigor and discipline.

TRINET: SWEET MUSIC—TARGETING OF PURCHASE READY BUYERS

TriNet (www.trinet.com), a leading provider of HR outsourcing services for small and medium-sized businesses, found that a face to face meeting with a sales consultant was a key step needed to push decision-making executives over the goal line. It built a strong base of thought leadership through several nurture campaigns, but wanted to motivate purchase-ready prospects to take the plunge.

To do this, TriNet devised a campaign with the call to action being a meeting with a TriNet salesperson—a significant commitment of time for any busy executive. The personal incentive: a free MP3 music player just before the upcoming holiday season.

This large incentive, combined with the call to action, meant that TriNet needed to ensure its targeting was accurate. Otherwise, it risked wasting money on a large number of respondents taking meetings simply for the free MP3 player. The real targets: decision makers who had previously engaged with TriNet but had NOT taken a meeting with a sales consultant.

To build that list of targets, TriNet turned to its database of prospects who had been nurtured with thought leadership campaigns. By segmenting on title, industry, and employee size, the ideal target list was constructed.

Using that list, TriNet launched a combined direct mail and e-mail campaign driving the prospects to a personalized site (www.mytrinet.com/prospectname). The mailer consisted of a small box containing MP3-player earphones to highlight the value of the offer and catch attention. Response activity from the prospects initiated a notification to the appropriate rep to begin scheduling the meeting before interest waned.

The campaign was highly successful in moving prospective buyers to the final stage of their buying process. Conversions to meetings increased by more than 20% over previous quarters and sales directly attributed to the campaign have generated more than 10 times the cost of the campaign.

Based on this success, the campaign has been repurposed as a key marketing asset in TriNet's nurturing process. Now, each potential buyer who becomes aware of TriNet through search, advertising, webinars, or whitepapers is entered into a nurturing campaign combining email and direct mail to build the case for TriNet's solutions. When interest (as measured by the prospect's digital body language) is detected 3 times, the incentive-based offer to take a meeting with a sales consultant is launched.

Without question, this level of marketing-operations discipline requires a new suite of skills and thought processes within the marketing organization, as well as strong executive-level support and engagement. However, the benefits of the digital body language discipline far outweigh the challenges of implementing the more structured approach to understanding, aggregating, and leveraging marketing data.

NATIONAL INSTRUMENTS: EXCHANGE OF VALUE FOR DIGITAL BODY LANGUAGE

National Instruments is a worldwide leader in software and hardware for scientists and engineers, with a very broad set of products and solutions serving nearly all industries and project types. Those products carry price tags anywhere between $100 and several million dollars. With more than 25,000 corporate customers and a Web presence that offers deeply detailed information on its products, National Instruments had both an incredible opportunity and a daunting challenge.

The company's marketing strategy fully revolves around its Web site. All direct marketing, search, ads, and tradeshows drive traffic to the Web site where the marketing team guides prospects through successive stages of engagement—from anonymous to known to understood.

To move visitors from anonymous to known, marketers at NI used Web forms to carefully execute an equitable exchange of value for key information on the site using a modular user profile as a building block. In exchange for presenting a two-minute video, it was acceptable to ask for an e-mail address and basic contact information. For a free trial download, a broader information request (buying cycle phase, budget, timeline, etc.) was appropriate.

To make these Web forms more valuable, the team ensured that all marketers could quickly manage which aspects of the modular user profile were required. Pre-population was used extensively to ensure visitors did not repeatedly answer the same question. Emphasis on global usability meant, for instance, that ZIP/postal codes were not required fields in geographies where that wasn't appropriate.

By increasing the percentage of known visitors, NI elevated the rich data from the Web visits to highly actionable information. For instance, nurture and follow-up communications catered to the areas of interest based on activity. By using digital body language to tailor communications this precisely, NI achieved open and click-through rates of 50 percent and 30 percent respectively—extremely high numbers compared to industry norms, and reflective of a strong engagement level with prospects

SALES AND MARKETING—A NEW RELATIONSHIP

The advent of digital body language not only spurs significant marketing-organization changes, it also initiates a transition of the relationship between marketing and sales. As every marketer (and sales professional) can attest, this relationship is perennially characterized by inherent conflict. Sales complains that marketing passes off leads with little or no value. Marketing complains that it passes large numbers of leads to sales, but sales does not properly follow up and pursue them.

By providing a clear and objective basis for understanding the qualification of a lead, digital body language rewrites many of the underlying assumptions and dynamics of this relationship. With agreement between the two organizations on what level of interest defines a quality lead, marketing can create and qualify defined numbers of objectively qualified leads. Meanwhile, sales can transition those leads into revenue. In this manner, a more objective and productive working relationship between marketing and sales becomes possible.

MEASURING MARKETING— A NEW OPPORTUNITY

As digital body language enables marketing to move further down the traditional funnel than has historically been possible, it also provides objectively measurable output in qualified leads. That improves the organization's ability to *objectively* measure marketing—an important achievement as the softer metrics (brand awareness, eyeballs, and site visits) continue to fall out of favor in organizations with complex sales processes.

Similarly, today's savvy marketers are far more interested in measurably driving buyer interest than yesterday's emphasis on the purely creative merits of a campaign. As marketing efforts become significantly more measurable, their relevance in guiding strategy and results increases significantly.

Marketers who adapt their thinking regarding marketing analytics and measurement to conform to these new realities will be able to use those analytics to guide their efforts and results in ways not previously possible. They will further both their own careers and the successes of the organizations they serve.

Exeros:
A Viral Contest Leads to the Creation of a University

Exeros was faced with an interesting challenge. As a small company with a revolutionary product in the master data management (MDM) industry, they had to get the word out and build awareness of their product. Confident that it had solved a 40 year old data management problem, they used a contest to prove their point. Beat your peers in data mapping with any technique or tool you wish, and win $2500, beat the machine and win $25,000.

As they began to build awareness of the contest, Exeros found a valuable ally in the organizer of DAMA—the largest conference in the industry. In an industry not known for excitement, the Exeros contest was just what was needed as a show highlight, and the contest was promoted to the conference list and the winner announced at a show lunch.

In combination with announcing the contest to their house list and embedding it in the email signature of all their employees, this allowed word of the contest to begin to spread. Independent data management forums and Yahoo groups began passing around word of the contest and soon the industry was well aware of both the contest and Exeros.

All interested participants were routed to a landing page where their information was captured and they were entered in the contest. On the day of the contest, a WebEx kicked off the contest with results due back in 2 hours. Over 200 industry experts competed for the prize, with no-one able to beat the Exeros machine. Coverage of the contest extended to 5 online publications that were highly relevant in the space, and Exeros became a known entity in the data management space.

Analyzing this success, Exeros realized that the viral contest had been a great win in getting awareness in the potential buying audience, but had not directly driven leads that were ready for sales. The challenge for Exeros was to help guide their prospective buyers from the "this is new" phase to the "I've got to get it" phase. To do this, the buyers needed to educate themselves on the challenges, approaches, and opportunities of a master data management project and where exactly a vendor like Exeros could help. Trade shows and Exeros-branded webinars were not as effective as needed due to travel costs and the assumed bias of a vendor webinar. The Exeros marketing team decided there was an opportunity to fill the knowledge gap in the market and use that as a way to attract potential buyers…and MDM University was born.

MDM University was launched as a separate brand (although with Exeros and their business partners identified as sponsors), with rich, valuable content, education at all needed depths throughout the lifecycle of an MDM project, and speakers from the industry. The MDM University was marketed through online ads and in trade publications.

By catering to the buyer's need for education, Exeros was able to attract a large audience of the key people in any buying decisions. Because MDM University was perceived to be vendor neutral, it was able to attract 5 times the number of attendees to a web seminar than Exeros or any of their vendor partners could on their own. Throughout the process, the educational choices of the University attendees were tracked to build a view of their interest areas and the phase in an MDM project they were at. Through sponsorship of MDM University communications, Exeros received tremendous brand exposure. When the Exeros sales team contacted a lead and introduced themselves as sponsors of MDM University, not only were they received as a highly respected and credible brand, but they were contacting prospective buyers at just the right phase of an MDM project.

FOUR

THE PROFILE OF
THE NEW BUYER

The first step in re-orienting one's thinking about a buyer's digital body language is observation. Without the ability to view and aggregate the telltale signs of digital body language, no marketer can use those signs to tailor their marketing messages and approaches. The marketer must understand the buyer along five key dimensions to leverage digital body language most effectively. They correspond to the key questions about a potential buyer that any sales professional would want to evaluate before initiating a sales cycle.

- How ready to buy is this person?

- What role does this person play compared to his colleagues?

- How interested is this person?

- What type of message best resonates with this person?

- What information on this person would be useful to obtain?

To understand the people they were selling to, professional salespeople found the answers to these key questions by observing the buyer's body language as they interacted. By observing that body language over time, the salesperson could subsequently guide the sales process.

Today, that challenge falls to the marketer, who must answer a similar set of questions solely by observing the

⇨ GET STARTED NOW

WEB SITES AND MEANINGFUL URLS

The easiest way to work with a Web site's insight into digital body language is through the use of meaningful URLs. Avoid storing multiple distinct information assets on one page or using incomprehensible strings as URLs. Instead, achieve the highest level of insight into the prospect's interests based solely on their path through your Web site. You can configure your site in this manner using popular content management systems.

---

buyer's digital body language, which can be discerned through four key elements:

- **Buyer's Stage**—At what stage of the buying process is the buyer? Are they just gaining awareness of leading solutions? Are they discovering options? Are they validating whether the solution is a viable option for them?

- **Buyer's Role**—Who is the prospective buyer? What role does he play in the buying group— technical evaluation, user representative, economic buyer? Is he a potentially strong advocate who can coach you internally? Is he looking for reasons to object or simply not interested?

- **Interest Level**—How interested is the buyer? Is the interest a transient phenomenon, or has he been interested for a long period of time? What are the hot buttons or sensitive issues?

- **Communication Preferences**—How does this buyer find his information? What types and styles of communication does he respond to? How frequently can you communicate with him without offending him?

Like a salesperson who is innately (perhaps even subconsciously) tuned into a buyer's physical body language, a marketer who can create a profile using a buyer's digital body language—a profile that provides consistent, predictive insight into buying intentions—is significantly more aware of the buyer's likelihood to take any particular action in the buying process. The challenge of marketing in this environment is to understand how to view and leverage the buyer's digital body language and optimize marketing efforts to each prospect.

UNDERSTANDING THE BUYER'S STAGE

To gain a clear understanding of what stage the prospective buyer is at, it helps to roughly categorize each prospect into one of three stages. By observing the buyer's interactions, we can make educated assumptions about how to categorize any potential buyer.

AWARENESS

The hallmarks of a buyer in the awareness phase are research and education. To group prospective buyers into this phase, marketers need insight into the specific and unique interactions that prospective buyers undertake to self-educate themselves on the market.

It might be nice if the operators of rich sources of information about what buyers are interested in—such as industry news sites and newsletters—would share their data with marketers. However, they are, understandably, quite hesitant to do so.

However, those sources can still yield useful digital body language in one meaningful way: the referred visitor. Web sites can detect what previous site referred the visitor to it through a link. This information starts to provide a very interesting picture of the prospective buyer.

As you can see, this visitor was referred to the Acme Web site by clicking on a Marketing Sherpa article about sales alignment. Clearly, this prospective buyer is exploring topics of interest around marketing, and educating himself on ideas and concepts.

⇨ *GET STARTED NOW*

WEB SITE HOT SPOTS

Most Web site designs feature areas that provide an extra level of insight into buyer behavior—such as sections with case studies or detailed product specifications. Make sure you can view this traffic by area, rather than by individual page. Tagging these pages with "meta" meaning will show you when a visitor views five case study pages and seven product pages—rather than 12 unique pages. This aggregation is immensely helpful in revealing a visitor's digital body language.

By carefully watching inbound referrals from relevant information sources, we can accumulate a valuable source of insight for marketers looking to understand their buyers' digital body language.

Awareness can also be more explicitly and proactively promoted, often in ways that exploit the creativity of today's best marketers. A viral marketing campaign, for example, is a great way to generate

Action	Details
	Referral from www.marketingsherpa.com
	www.acme.com/SalesAlignment
	www.acme.com/CaseStudies
	Download Form: Case Studies

Figure 7: Digital body language showing a prospect being referred from an industry site.

awareness by blending a (usually) humorous message with a smaller message to build marketing awareness about the organization's solution.

Action	Details
	Referral from www.youtube.com/ViralVideo
	www.acme.com/ViralLandingPage
	Download Form: Trial Download
	Email Open: Thanks for Registering

Figure 8: Digital body language of a viral marketing campaign on You-Tube leading to a trial download.

To derive the greatest possible insight that a viral campaign can provide, it should be structured to drive interested recipients to take action that is visible and measurable by the sponsoring marketer. However, burdensome processes, such as filling out a form, can stifle the spread of the viral campaign. With Web analytics, however, we can leverage a more passive way to understand the digital body language of buyers who have learned about the solution through the viral campaign.

Perhaps the best way to measure the impact of a viral campaign is to create a purpose-built microsite that is specific to that campaign. Any traffic that hits the microsite is directly caused by the viral campaign. Those microsite visitors are showing the digital body language of a prospect at the awareness phase of their buying process.

At the awareness phase, it may not be possible to capture individual names and contact information of prospective buyers—and that's a mental hurdle for traditional marketers. However, as you begin to build active profiles, understanding which companies they are arriving from (via the referred visitor data) is a critical first step, especially in complex B2B sales environments.

Today's Web analytics are generally able to provide insight on which companies are visiting the microsite. If this is driven by a viral campaign promoting awareness, it indicates that an individual at that company is in this phase of their buying process.

Company	Visitors	Pages
Endeca	4	14
TriNet	3	12
ADP	3	11
Cognos	2	9

Figure 9: Activity from companies showing a buying event may be happening in those companies.

Fortunately, many other marketing techniques used in awareness-building are much less anonymous. For instance, Web-based seminars (webinars) focused on thought leadership can focus on target audiences outside of the marketer's current prospect database. When a registration comes in from outside the "house list," that prospect is now identified. Their registration for a webinar also identifies them as being in the awareness phase of their buying cycle.

The art of marketing using a buyer's digital body language is to ensure that this profile is highly usable in aggregated and single form. That means information such as webinar registrations can be correlated with the other aspects of digital body language previously mentioned to provide validity and confirm its predictive value.

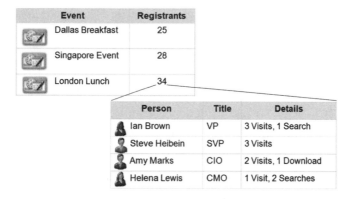

Figure 10: Marketing techniques such as events can be tied into online activity information to add to the prospects' digital body language.

DISCOVERY

In the discovery phase, prospective buyers move from self-education about a market to active exploration and discovery of potential solutions. This phase can be a make-or-break inflection point for the marketer because this is the point where the solution is either investigated further or eliminated from further consideration. This is also a highly time-critical phase because a latent business pain has been escalated and those who are tasked with solving it are actively motivated to find a solution.

The first step: look for signs that involve solution discovery and light research. And the best place to look here is with search media -both paid and organic. The fact is, most prospective buyers seeking solutions in a particular product/service category will, as a first step, perform search queries on Google, Yahoo!, or other search engines that reflect the manner in which they have categorized that business challenge in their own mind.

Marketers are increasingly turning to search engine optimization strategies and search engine marketing campaigns to target prospective buyers precisely at this discovery stage of the buying cycle. They are engaged in a continuous battle to ensure that whatever search term the prospect uses leads him to either a sponsored-search advertisement or an organic listing for the vendor's solutions.

The key, of course, is to know what search terms buyers are using to reach your site. This provides a crucial aspect of the prospective buyer's digital body language. Simply by seeing the precise term or phrase the buyer entered into the search engine to reach the corporate site and discover the solution offered, the marketer can better identify the buyer's interests and more deeply understand which stage the buyer is at in the sales cycle.

▷ GET STARTED NOW

E-MAIL AND RSS GIVE ADDED INSIGHT

Really Simple Syndication (RSS) is a popular way to distribute content on the Web—in news readers or as components of "gadget" pages such as iGoogle. Integrate a relevant RSS feed into your outbound e-mail initiatives and watch click-through rates to get a better sense of your recipients' interests—which may be slightly different than the main content of the message.

Search Term	Visitors
Google Demand Generation	12
Google Marketing Automation	9
Google Campaign Management	6
Google Lead Management	4

Figure 11: Overall trends in digital body language can provide insights into what prospects are seeking when they discover your solutions.

In a similar way, tradeshows are a time-tested way for buyers to identify vendors that may be able to resolve the buyer's business challenge/pain. They provide a unified forum for engaging with multiple vendors in one location—a level of efficiency that buyers find compelling. Many marketers invest extensively in their tradeshow exhibits. In doing so, they capture lists of hundreds or even thousands of contacts.

Of course, as every sales professional knows, tradeshow attendees are rarely prospects ready to purchase a solution in the short term. However, tradeshow attendance does indicate—at minimum—that the prospective buyer is gaining awareness of a particular industry segment. Interacting with your organization or responding to follow-up campaigns may indicate a prospect in the discovery phase of their buying process.

Properly, fully, and effectively leveraging these digital body language signs requires marketers to intelligently aggregate, integrate, and synthesize the prospect's offline

> **⇨ GET STARTED NOW**
>
> ### RICH-MEDIA ASSETS AS HOT SPOTS
>
> Flash, video, and other rich-media assets can play a central role in your Web site strategy by keeping your prospects engaged and educated. If the rich-media asset runs longer than a minute, make sure you tie it to your Web tracking so that you can see whether a viewer viewed part, most, or all of the asset. This depth-of-viewing metric provides excellent insight into interest levels.

and online behavior data. Without this linkage, it is difficult or impossible to understand whether a prospect is a tradeshow visitor who was motivated by booth giveaway, or if a prospect is, after learning about your solution, beginning to research it more fully.

VALIDATION

The solution validation phase typically leads a prospect to display very distinct digital body language to what is seen at other stages of the buying process. Prospective buyers are much more focused in their information-seeking process, attempting to determine whether a short-listed solution can meet the specific needs of their business challenge. The digital body language includes signs of objection-based research, deep technical evaluation, solution trial, economic investigation, and solution comparison.

Fortunately, these activities translate into relatively easily discernible clues for marketers who know what to look for. In fact, many solution-validation activities take place on or surrounding the vendor's own Web site. Many organizations see heightened activity with their detailed product information and evaluation guides. Repeated visits by multiple individuals from the buyer's organization are another strong indication that a prospect has reached this stage.

Another ideal source of digital body language in the validation phase is the terms that prospective buyers use searching on Google, Yahoo!, or other sites. As he moves from discovery to validation, the searching style steadily evolves from a broad wandering to a much more focused path. These terms can provide great insight into the buyer's stage and intentions. Looking for clues such as whether the search term represented the general pain, the solution category, or the vendor's name can give a clue as to where in the buying process the prospect is.

Prospective buyers in the validation stage also seek out significant literature (such as industry articles and analyst reports) on blogs or Web sites. Most often, these "research searches" center on comparative or evaluative information.

For marketers, the changes in the buyer's digital body language present important opportunities to streamline and facilitate the buyer's access to appropriate industry information. It's essential to clearly understand how the prospect uses each piece of information. By gaining that clear understanding of who looks at what, when it's looked at, and what that action means, marketers begin to gradually piece together the buyer's digital body language of the validation stage.

Action	Details
BLOG	Blog Referral: Comparing Demand Generation Systems
	Webinar Registration: Demo
	www.acme.com/ProductDetails
	Download Form: Free Trial
	www.acme.com/HelpDocumentation

Figure 12: Digital body language of a prospect in the validation phase shows a deep interest in product details, a free trial, and documentation.

UNDERSTANDING EACH BUYER'S ROLE

To properly interpret digital body language, marketers must first understand the range of buyer roles and match them to different individuals in the buyer organization. A sales professional carefully observes the room to see who defers to whom, who asks what questions, and who is interested in what topics to understand who is acting in what role. It's the same for the marketer who is filtering through the data of digital body language.

Different sales methodologies use varying terms that have subtly different definitions, and each vendor will use some variation of these roles, depending on their own sales model and value proposition. However, at a high level, there are typically four major buyer roles that factor into most complex sales situations: economic, user, technical, and coach. Using digital body language, the marketer must isolate the different participants and assign them to one of these roles so that messages can be appropriately crafted and tailored to each individual—just as if they were physically present in the same room.

THE ECONOMIC BUYER

This buyer is the gatekeeper to the budget and evaluates projects from an ROI perspective. Some of the most relevant aspects of digital body language—from a marketing perspective—are case studies, client examples, and financial models that showcase the ROI of the vendor's solution, marketing assets that are easy to identify and

Action	Details
Google	Search: "acme pricing"
	www.acme.com/ProductLevelComparisons
	Download Form: ROI Calculator
	Email Click-Through: MegaCorp Case Study
	www.acme.com/CaseStudy_FinanceCo
	www.acme.com/CaseStudy_BuilderCo
	Download Form: Analyst Review

Figure 13: Digital body language of an economic buyer shows a focus on ROI and case studies in order to understand the value of the considered solution.

define. Web analytics make it easy to quickly identify the digital body language of an economic buyer.

It is more challenging to identify economic buyers because they are also interested in the longer-term aspects of a project, such as total cost of ownership (TCO). That can lead them to investigate such things as the vendor's viability, the makeup of the management team, or the likelihood that a solution vendor may be acquired. Economic buyers often examine these facets from a perspective of risk. If the vendor goes out of business, loses a key executive, or is acquired, they must anticipate the effects on the project.

THE USER BUYER

This buyer's role is to evaluate the operational impact of the proposed solution—how will it be used on a daily basis and who will it affect? Their information needs

Action	Details
	Download Form: Free Trial
	www.acme.com/ProductDocumentation
	Customer Community: Signed Up
	Email Click-Through: Tips & Tricks
	Blog: Acme Afficionados

Figure 14: Digital body language of a user buyer shows an interest in the customer community, and experimentation with a product in order to better understand the user experience.

are much different than the economic buyer's and will betray a distinct digital body language. He generally explores the hands-on aspects of the vendor's Web site—such as trials, demos, user documentation, downloads, and similar assets.

User buyers also like to consult with peers through user groups and community sites to learn about the experiences and gain the perspectives of others who have implemented the proposed solution. Because their investigations can be quite extensive and granular, they often present a rich trove of digital body language data. However, marketers must be careful about the extent and frequency with which they ask the user buyer for the same information. Marketers should carefully capture information on the user buyer's investigation and quickly integrate it into the buyer's profile—all in a way that does not impede access to needed information.

THE TECHNICAL BUYER

The technical buyer brings specialized expertise to the evaluation team and analyzes the proposed solution from the perspective of feasibility. He is much more likely to devote much of his investigative time to understanding specifications, technical details, implementation and integration challenges, and expected project challenges in any transition to the new solution.

In many instances, technical buyers don't have ready access to the required information so they may spend a more significant amount of time searching for information. Well-executed search engine optimization techniques can enable the marketer to identify the technical buyer based on objection-oriented searches. If the solution on offer involves a product that can be tried or demonstrated, the technical buyer is very likely to lead or play a major role in such a trial.

THE COACH

In traditional sales cycles, the coach in the buying process is often easily identifiable in the room through his strong personal relationships with

Action	Details
	Download Form: Case Studies
	www.acme.com/CaseStudy_FinanceCo
	Email Forward: Case Study - FinanceCo
	Email Forward: Case Study - ManufacturingCo
	Tradeshow Attendance: With 3 colleagues

Figure 16: Digital body language of a coach shows a trend of internal promotion of a solution.

peers and the vendor along with a palpable eagerness to see your solution implemented. However, even in the online realm, marketers can interpret a site visitor's digital body language that allows them to identify potential coaches earlier in the process.

Perhaps the clearest indicator of the enthusiasm that coaches bring to buying cycles is the internal propagation of your messages. Forwarding e-mails to peers and executives within the organization—or downloading marketing material targeted at facilitating this type of internal promotion—are both excellent indicators that the prospect can play the coach's role in the buying process.

UNDERSTANDING THE BUYER'S INTEREST LEVEL

Now that we understand the roles/categories that different participants in the buying process have, we want to understand the intensity of their interest. Once again, digital body language—like its physical counterpart—can yield solid, predictive clues about interest levels. First, it's important to recognize that it is entirely appropriate and expected for a prospect's interest level to evolve and change over time, depending on the internal dynamics and events at the prospect's organization. There are three main dimensions that help us quantify the prospect's current level of interest.

RECENCY

The timing of events in a buying cycle is as important as the events themselves, which makes it important to understand prospect-profile data from a temporal perspective. The same download or page load can mean very different things at different times in the sales cycle. For instance, the download of a very basic, introductory data sheet after several months of interest may indicate that a new buyer has joined the evaluation team.

What's more, the freshness of the data you receive to analyze is critical. The same data, three months, three weeks, or even three days out of date, is significantly less relevant to understanding a prospect's interest in engaging in a sales conversation. It's critical to ensure that all data on prospects flows in real time into a comprehensive profile of prospects, and is available in an equally real-time fashion.

FREQUENCY

How often does the prospective buyer engage with your marketing message? The answer contains an important element of digital body language and is a key indicator of his current level of interest in your solution. As you use digital body language to evaluate prospective buyers and understand their roles and stages in the buying process, it is also important to monitor their patterns of engagement over time. For instance, a sudden spike in activity tells a very different story than a steady pattern of low-level interest, even though the aggregate level of activity over time may be the same.

An accurate profile of interaction frequency requires you to efficiently capture and integrate all interaction points—online or offline. The accurate assessment of interaction frequency can only be achieved by aggregating all relevant interaction points within one comprehensive prospect profile.

Depth

In most sales cycles, the depth of engagement by the prospect is, in many ways, the most accurate and actionable metric of a prospect's interest. The question is simply: How deeply does the prospect interact with your assets and resources? This depth can vary significantly and betray vastly different levels of interest—from "tire-kicker" to committed buyer. Naturally, the more deeply a prospect engages by acquiring more of your content, the more interested that prospect is and the more open he is to engagement with your sales organization. Likewise, if a prospect engages more deeply with one area of content than another, it clearly shows an interest leaning in that direction.

Too often, however, this dimension of the prospect is not accurately captured. A seamless tie between outbound marketing and the Web site is needed to ensure a proper capture of that depth of response. It can also require additional up-front efforts to ensure that marketing assets, even such self-contained assets as Flash demos, are correctly configured to accurately reflect the depth of usage by a visitor. For example, the difference between a buyer who viewed a Flash demo passively for a mere 30 seconds, and a buyer who interacted with the Flash demo in numerous ways over a five-minute period is clearly significant.

KADIENT: SEARCH REBRANDING LEADS TO GREATER INSIGHTS

Kadient is a leading vendor of sales-knowledge, RFP, and proposal-generation software, using a free trial strategy that enables buyers to better experience the product's value and positively compare Kadient to other possible solutions. In order to reflect their evolution from a niche, premise-based solution to a broader software-as-a-service solution, they undertook an ambitious rebranding from its prior name—Pragmatech. In doing so, they realized that a significant effort would be needed to ensure that the search engine optimization work they had put into the Pragmatech name would carry over to the new name and new URL. They ended up, however, realizing some much deeper insights into how their buyers found them.

As they optimized their search efforts to the new name, the Kadient team made careful observations of the digital body language of the prospect who found their way to their site and also the ways in which the broader universe sought information on sales challenges. Kadient quickly realized that they had been optimizing against terms such as "sales effectiveness", which reflected their solution, but the broader market was seeking help with "sales coaching".

Armed with this insight, the Kadient team realized that they could tap into a new opportunity. By explaining to prospective buyers, who were searching for "sales coaching" why they should think about the more than just a glib guy in a suit giving an inspirational session, Kadient was able to engage with a much broader audience and make them aware of the Kadient solution.

By analyzing the digital body language of its prospects, Kadient quickly identified a broad new opportunity for market awareness and education, and has begun to engage with buyers who may not have even initially realized that the problem they were wrestling with could be solved by a solution such as Kadient's.

COMMUNICATION PREFERENCE

Digital body language holds the key to a marketer's understanding a prospective buyer's stage in their buying process, what role he plays, and how interested he is. Similarly, it is no less important to understand how the prospective buyer prefers to receive information they require to make their decisions.

Failing to understand these communications preferences makes it unnecessarily difficult to have messages reach prospects and ensure they are received and read at the right times. The three aspects of communication preferences that digital body language can provide insight on are media type, style, and frequency.

MEDIA TYPE

Although each stage of the buying process is characterized by a set of marketing vehicles and media types that are used more frequently, marketers must also pay attention to what vehicles and media that buyers prefer. Some buyers want information through RSS feed readers, while others prefer e-mail. Some buyers prefer direct mail but others want podcasts. Some buyers will attend tradeshows while others are avid readers of industry analyst reports.

Capture the digital body language of your prospective buyers across all media types and communication vehicles to ensure you understand each prospect's buying signals—regardless of where they are shown. At the same time, you want to ensure you can connect with each individual involved in the buying process.

Ideally, marketers want to identify this preference early in the buying process. That helps ensure that as buyers progress through the solution discovery and validation phases, that marketing messages have a better likelihood of being favorably received and that marketers are well-informed of their buyer's communication preferences.

STYLE

As with media types, marketers will find that different prospects appreciate different styles of communication. Some prefer rich graphical communications, but others prefer a more straightforward text-only style. Many prospects like a writing voice that is more educational, while others demonstrably respond better to sales-oriented messages.

Although subtle, this style preference is likely to shift as the prospect progresses through the buying process. However, it will always be skewed to his personal preferences for inbound vendor communication. This is a data-driven phenomenon that can be objectively understood by observing their digital body language as they interact with your marketing messages throughout the buying process.

FREQUENCY

The frequency with which marketers communicate with the prospective should—appropriately—show large shifts throughout the buying process. As the prospect becomes more familiar with and engaged with the vendor organization, their comfort increases. A more frequent communication style is more likely to be welcomed without leading the prospect to abruptly disengage.

Monitor a prospect's progression through the sales cycle by profiling both the communication frequency and the associated responses. By using this metric to better understand their level of engagement, you can begin to see whether the current frequency is properly calibrated.

While the level of acceptable communication frequency changes during a buying process, it is by no means an airtight indicator to guide communications with any one individual prospect. It is, however, very useful to monitor the digital body language of prospects at each stage of the process based on the frequency of communication. For instance, if the digital body language shows an attenuation of interest when communication frequency

CAP/CAPAF: Understanding Constituent Interest

The Center for American Progress and its sister organization Center for American Progress Action Fund are think tanks focused on raising awareness on a variety of issues, from health and government to the environment and foreign policy. Their product is the distribution and adoption of their ideas. CAP/CAPAF markets issues-focused events, policy papers, and online publications to sub groups of their overall constituent base with an interest in that particular topic and their level of influence. As such, they need to be very in tune with the interest areas and focus of their constituents.

To gain this insight, they turned to digital body language to provide a deeper understanding of the interest areas and depth of their audience. Each person in the audience manages their own preferences indicating interest in two dimensions. Firstly, the topics of interest; Iraq, economy, environments, etc, are selected, and for each topic of interest a depth (somewhat interested to very interested) is selected. Secondly, the user controls their subscription to an array of regularly generated products including daily cartoons, weekly newsletters, monthly reports, and ad hoc alerts.

With this understanding of the constituents' stated interests, CAP/CAPAF manages their outbound communications. However, in analyzing their data, they look beyond this to understand the actual interest patterns shown by individuals as compared to their stated interests. For example, if a constituent displays an interest in the mortgage crisis, CAP/CAPAF would provide related links to other housing issues or other domestic policy topics in order to better understand the drivers of the constituent interest.

In communicating with their constituents, CAP/CAPAF uses their understanding of the actual interest patterns of their constituents to ensure that they market each issue-focused event, newsletter, or action campaign to the right sub group of their constituents based on actual, current interests. The goal is to increase the quality of the relationship between CAP/CAPAF and the constituent by providing more of what they want and less of what that person thinks is clutter. Sending less email helps the remaining communications stand out more.

is higher, it indicates that it may be beneficial to recalibrate communications at that stage to other buyers in the future.

THE AGGREGATED PROSPECT PROFILE

A marketer's ability to more fully leverage digital body language and understand where buying organizations are in the buying process is predicated on a comprehensive real-time profile of each buyer's digital body language—including the ability to see all aspects of digital body language, across all relevant media types, in real time. Without it, the marketer is blind to telltale signs of who he is marketing to and what that person would be interested in learning.

At each communication touchpoint, marketers must first think about how that touchpoint and its response can be monitored in ways that provide richer insight into

SYBASE: BUYER PROFILING FOR MICRO SEGMENT

For one of its key data-management products, Sybase IQ, Sybase needed to engage with a specific set of its customers: "the data elite"—people who needed fast response times in a solution to tackle extremely high volumes of data. The Sybase IQ product leveraged a new approach to data storage and querying that resulted in performance improvements of many orders of magnitude. The target buyers, however, in many cases were not aware that such a solution was possible, and may have been grudgingly purchasing ever larger hardware in order to tackle the problem.

To connect with this audience, the Sybase team leveraged the naturally competitive nature of administrators of huge volumes of data, and their desire to compare themselves against their peers. The campaign targeted a scrubbed list of existing Sybase contacts and asked them for information on the extreme challenges they were tackling—data volume, response time, or both. Based on their answers, one of three cartoon icons guided them through an information-gathering process where they were ranked as a Pro, an Expert, or Elite by comparing them to their peers.

With this basic knowledge, the campaign guided them through five stages—from collecting basic information through to fully engaged, through sharing thought leadership from industry gurus and case studies of similar professionals becoming corporate heroes through delivering massive performance increases. At each step, the content and detailed information provided was tightly matched to the individual's biggest challenge and rank. By observing their interactions with available content, the campaign transitioned the customer from one buying stage to the next.

By cultivating that competitive spirit among database experts as to who tackles the larger data challenge, Sybase engaged with the "data elite" in ways that enabled the company to better understand who would be an ideal audience for the product. By catering to this competitive spirit, Sybase was also able to develop the opportunity to present to them possible solutions, that they had never thought possible, to a very real challenge they were having.

the digital body language. How will I track this and what will tracking it reveal? What's more, each investment in understanding digital body language must build on preceding efforts in the sales cycle to create an increasingly comprehensive profile.

Once the profile is created, the marketer can analyze it to uncover the relevant insights into the buying process and decide how the course of communications should proceed. That requires the individual insights in the prospect profiles to be distilled to a granular level that is actionable. This is where lead scoring becomes critical.

FIVE

THE SCORING
IMPERATIVE

When a sales professional leads a sales call with an important prospect, he gathers a wealth of data. To his trained eye, each frown or furrowed brow conveys an important message he ignores at his peril. The slouching postures, crossed arms, raised eyebrows, and deferring glances all demonstrate the power dynamics of the attendees. The sales representative's ability to detect and decode these many different data points is a predicate of his success.

That same challenge exists in the online world as well: understanding the subtle, implicit communications cues from buyers—the digital body language. Fortunately for marketers, the volume of granular data points that a prospective buyer presents is staggeringly large. The art lies in the marketer's ability to draw meaning from that data and build meaningful predictive models that reveal, rank, and categorize the qualified buyers. In digital body language, this means lead scoring.

⇨ *GET STARTED NOW*

HOT OR NOT: THE BASICS OF SCORING

The smartest way to start scoring leads is with a simple, basic approach. Look at raw activity (such as total pages viewed or total visits) to calculate a basic implicit score. Use simple data (such as title, industry, revenue) to determine a basic explicit score. Together, these two scores yield a reliable indication of interest. Only after you have your sales team focused on good, solid leads should you start to tweak and optimize the scoring algorithm.

Through lead scoring, marketers aggregate, process, categorize, and digest the wealth of profile data and present clear and accurate conclusions regarding who the hot prospects are. Lead scoring starts with the answers to three important questions:

1. What Dimension Are You Analyzing?

Are you evaluating the buyer's role or the phase of the buying process? Each of the different dimensions for gauging buyer interest discussed in Chapter 4 requires a different approach. Merely attempting to integrate all of these relevant aspects into a single dimension will create major frustration.

The most common dimensions to score against are the four main areas of prospect profiling: the stage in the buying process, the buyer's role, the demonstrated or expressed level of interest, and communication preferences. Each of these has its own nuances and challenges, but collectively, the key approaches in scoring will become apparent.

Figure 17: The common dimensions on which scoring is done.

Once a prospect universe is scored along multiple dimensions, it can often be instructive to combine multiple dimensions, such as role and interest level, into a multi-dimensional view that provides additional insight into targeted buyers.

2. ARE YOU USING A SPECTRUM OR CATEGORIZATION?

Lead scoring implies a spectrum of scores, continually increasing as a prospect increases his engagement and activity. Although this can be true in many instances,

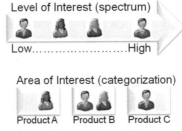

Figure 18: Spectrums and categorization for scoring.

other lead-scoring approaches can also be helpful in categorizing and aggregating prospects into one or more groups, such as topic of most interest, or stage in buying process. Spectrum-based and categorization-based scoring routines require substantially different approaches, so upfront clarity can be beneficial in achieving desired results

⇨ *GET STARTED NOW*

LEADS TO SALES: A HOT LIST

Handing off scored leads ("marketing-qualified leads") should start with a simple, effective process. A nightly e-mail "hot list" of leads—names with good activity or good scores—is a great start. Sales reps will still rely on their intuition to determine which individuals to call, so airtight accuracy isn't necessarily the goal. By sending the hot list, you enable sales to gain insights into their prospects' digital body language before they make their initial contact.

3. TIME

In almost all situations, time is an exceedingly relevant component of a scoring algorithm. For motivated buyers, factors such as a prospect's level of interest or stage in the buying cycle can move quickly—even in the span of a few weeks. Conversely, a prospect's role in the process or communication preference are far less likely to change quickly—or at all—over time. When scoring for longer term strategies such as communication type and messaging choice, it's key to ensure that the knowledge of this buyer's preferences are maintained over the long haul. The impact of time on the dimension you are scoring is critical to the accuracy and predictability of scoring algorithms

WHAT DOES IT ALL MEAN?: EVALUATING DIGITAL BODY LANGUAGE

Once marketers understand the dimensions they are evaluating—spectrum or a categorization—and the corresponding effects of time, they can begin to determine how to evaluate prospects through a five-step process.

1. MARKETING ASSET EVALUATION

Evaluate the insight into the dimension that each marketing asset can provide. A thorough cataloguing of marketing assets—and the nuances of digital body language they can reveal—often highlights surprising insights. At each point that prospects interact with the organization, ask the following questions:

- In what ways can a prospect interact with this marketing asset? For example, an e-mail can be opened, forwarded, and clicked-through. Each of those interactions can be performed multiple times.

- What does each interaction (likely) reveal about that prospect? Does it provide insight into their area of interest? Does it declare how they like to be communicated with? Can it show what calls-to-action catch their eye?

- Can the marketing asset provide different insights if aggregated into a larger group? As any statistician would agree, one individual response to a monthly newsletter may not show much actionable insight. But a sustained level of some activity over a long period of time shows a prospect who is maintaining awareness of an industry or a solution. What's more, multiple prospects interacting with the same asset and responding similarly create a heightened level of validity for the predictive properties of that asset.

- Can the marketing asset provide different insight if broken down into smaller units? A Web site visit of 10 pages shows a certain level of interest, but breaking the site down into categories of content affords a greater level of insight into what type of buyer the prospect is, or what area they are interested in. For example, if the 10 pages were technical product specifications on Product A, we could safely conclude that the visitor is a technical buyer, interested in Product A.

Assign a numeric score for each interaction with a marketing asset that a buyer can have, reflecting the significance you assign to that buyer's action. Generally, a scale of 0-100 is instructive, so perhaps each action can be worth 5-20 points.

As each marketing asset is catalogued and understood, larger trends will emerge concerning the marketing assets as a whole. Seek commonalities among different assets and bundle together into larger categories those assets that generate similar insights into the prospect's digital body language. Remember, this scoring is generally not cumulative. For example, if the marketer assigns a value of 10 points (out of a maximum of 100) to a white paper download, it would be inappropriate to conclude that 10 white papers mean the prospect is valued at a perfect score of 100 points.

For each category of overlapping items, decide on a maximum score for that category. This means that the contribution of individual items in that category can only add up to a "category maximum." This allows each item to contribute individually to its full extent without improperly skewing the score if the prospect is unusually active in one particular category.

▷ *GET STARTED NOW*

EXPLICIT AND IMPLICIT SCORING SPLIT FOR BETTER INSIGHT

Once your basic scoring is in place, it's a good idea to split that score in two: explicit (title, role, revenue) and implicit (level of interest, visits, marketing response). Even a very rough view of this data gives sales reps a good way to prioritize their leads. Present both scores so they can quickly see who is the right person and who is interested.

BUILDING YOUR MATRIX

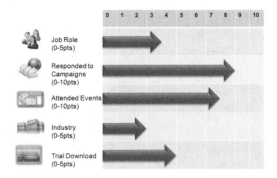

Figure 19: Building a matrix for scoring prospects based on a few criteria.

For each marketing asset, identify the dimensions that matter most to your lead scoring. They might be job role, purchase timeframe, frequency and/or recency of Web site visits, location, or industry. Then assign scores to each dimension. For instance, a job title can earn 1-5 points. A VP title earns three points, but a manager title only earns 1. A New England location earns 2 points, but a West Coast location earns 5. Finally, aggregate the point totals and create "break points" that categorize a lead into an A, B, C, or D grouping. This helps you understand which assets generate which responses from different roles in the sales cycle.

TIME-BASED MODELING

Once scores for each marketing-asset interaction have been allocated, it's time to evaluate how to handle the

Sourcefire: Open Source Marketing Ecosystem

As a leader in network security solutions, Sourcefire had both an opportunity and a challenge. Their freely available and popular open source SNORT® intrusion prevention system drove significant awareness and interest, but for their sales team to be most effective, they needed to engage with only the leads who were likely to purchase a commercial offering. To enable this, Sourcefire's marketing team had to enable prospective buyers to progress through the maturity spectrum and identify those who were ready for sales engagement.

Search engine strategies targeted buyers at all phases of the buying cycle, with education offered to those searching for category-related terms and deeper demos and comparisons targeted at those searching for Sourcefire or a competitor directly. To start the process, Sourcefire created an education-heavy web experience. For those new to the category, analyst reports, case studies, demos, webcasts, and thought leadership were provided for little more than a small amount of information. This enabled Sourcefire to establish themselves in the prospects' minds as a leader in the space, and engage in the start of an ongoing dialog, while at the same time guiding the prospects' understanding and awareness of what matters most in security.

When engaged, a rich profile on interests and level of engagement enabled both the scoring of leads and the nurturing of those not yet ready for sales. A four category scoring system looked at marketing source, site activity, title, and company profile in order to score and categorize leads.

With leads categorized in A, B, C, and D leads, the Sourcefire team did an interesting thing; A and B leads were immediately handed to sales, but the entire lead funnel was opened to them. Sales professionals would occasionally notice a D lead in a key account, and use the non-qualified lead as an opportunity to begin a relationship that would be valuable when the lead matures to a later stage.

Leads that were not picked up were nurtured over time, and with dashboard metrics on lead population by level, they were moved slowly down the funnel. Each nurturing campaign was measured on its ability to transition leads between the stages. With this overall marketing structure in place, the Sourcefire marketing team proudly points to two key data points as measures of its success; their sales team has stopped screaming for more leads, and most recently they achieved year-over-year quarterly revenue growth of 42% in 2Q08 over 2Q07. Both of which, of course, are great accomplishments for any marketing organization.

element of time. There are three main approaches to modeling time in a lead-scoring algorithm:

- **Historical All-Time**—This simply ignores the impact of timing from the scoring algorithm, and the prospect's full history is used to calculate a score—whether the activity spans weeks, months, or years. Data collected months or years ago is considered equal to data collected as recently as yesterday. This philosophy should only apply when time is not seen as a factor in gauging prospect interest or where lengthy intervals of data provide more insight than brief spikes in activity. For instance, communication preference is a dimension where historical all-time scoring is very relevant because it is disconnected from particular interests or ongoing projects that might drive purchase decisions..

- **Single Point of Interest**—This approach captures one defined and recent point of interest, excluding all prior data points to clearly highlight the key point of interest. This algorithm looks within a minimum timeframe (e.g. 30 days) for a point of interest. All scoring is limited to profile data collected within that minimum timeframe. This approach can be useful in identifying specific buying events, or interest upticks using scoring, but since it is limited to recent events, no historical profile of a prospect is built. Think of as more like a snapshot than a timeline.

- **Recency and Relevance**—This model leverages the entire data history but applies a positive weighting to events that are more recent. All historical events and interactions are captured, but over time are subject to different "half-lives" to reduce their value over time—sometimes to a fraction of their original value and sometimes even to zero. Scores for recent events are added without any aging/decrease. This approach is ideal for prospecting models where a buyer's interests may change over time.

CATEGORIZATION OF OUTPUT

If your dimension-scoring results in a categorization, it can be tempting to conclude that this scoring algorithm is not as effective as a spectrum. Most marketers, however, who build a scoring algorithm that segments prospects into a number of categories, find it very effective to use the above heuristics for each of the categories. Handling time is generally identical across all categories, as are the general sizes of each increment of scoring (to allow balance and easier comparisons). Each category is then scored uniquely, and the category with the maximum score is retained as the selected category.

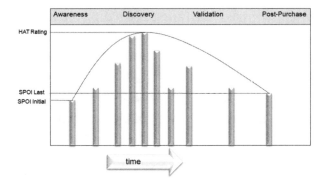

Figure 20: Interest over time of a prospect shows numerous points of interest throughout the buying process. Comparing HAT and SPOI ratings gives a clearer view of actual interest level.

A buyer's interest has a natural variability over time. It can be helpful to analyze these variations to identify statistically significant upticks in buyer behavior. By comparing a SPOI to a Historical All Time score, you can see when a prospect is flashing stronger "buy" signals.

Even in a dimension with a spectrum of scores, such as interest level, most marketers find it useful to group the scores into A, B, C (or hot, warm, or cold) to improve coordination of differentiated processes for prospects in each category.

PROCESS DEFINITION OR HAND-OFF

Each prospect is a dynamic entity within his or her own world. Interest levels in a solution may rise and fall. Transient internal events that can drive buying processes come and go. But the effectiveness of your sales team is—more than ever before—driven by how accurately your marketing team identifies the nuances of digital body language that correspond with these peaks of interest or buying signals—and the proceeding to quickly deliver the right information to that prospect.

As a result, process has an unusually prominent role in lead scoring. Sometimes, your scoring process will lead you to guide the prospect back to a nurture cycle. At times, it will guide you to change the topics, media, or approach that you use to communicate information to the prospect. Other times, it will hand the prospect off to a field sales team for further engagement. Regardless, a lead-scoring process is only as valuable and effective as the hand-off process that it supports.

What makes this important and relevant is that hand-off points may not be entirely driven by a single dimension of scoring. Consider, for example, the handoff of a lead from marketing to sales at a point where marketing has determined the lead is qualified. Ideally, marketing and sales agree on the definition of what it means to be "qualified" and marketing works to create "marketing-qualified leads" (MQLs) that it passes to sales who accepts the leads and begins to work them.

An MQL, however, might not fall along a single dimension such as interest level or role. It might, in fact, be a combination of more than one of these. For instance, sales may require a lead to exhibit a level of interest above 50, a person interested in Product A, and a certain role before it accepts the lead. As a result, the process handoff has to reflect multiple lead dimensions in the scoring.

ANALYSIS, OPTIMIZATION, AND REFINEMENT

Scoring and qualifying leads along multiple dimensions is an ongoing, evolving process—a sort of simultaneous equation. To enable it to evolve in an optimal fashion, we must measure what's working and what isn't so that optimizations and refinements can be made. The first step: understand the endpoints that the marketer is seeking to shape. Whether it's an increase in sales-accepted leads (SALs) through better qualification, an increase in campaign effectiveness through better prospect targeting, or greater market share through real-time identifica-

TERRACOTTA: LEAD SCORING A BUYER'S JOURNEY IN OPEN SOURCE

As a leading open-source software company, Terracotta has a challenge that most marketers would gladly choose to manage: too many leads. However, that wealth can create problems when you only have a few direct sales professionals. Those leads were generated from interest in a very strong, full-featured, open-source version of its software —but which were ideal prospects to target for commercial service offerings?

The Terracotta marketing team turned to lead scoring to allow them to understand the process their buyers went through in understanding and evaluating their products. First, they categorized the buyer's journey into a path called RESITD—Recognize, Evaluate, Sample, Integrate, Test, Deploy. Lead scoring was used to categorize each buyer in this buying path. The key metrics of each phase differed, depending on the likely approach a buyer would have:

- Recognition: Awareness metrics such as the number of visits

- Evaluate: Reading of introductory documents on Terracotta benefits

- Sample: Downloading of the Terracotta open source product

- Integrate: Forum activity, application-specific integration documents, or downloading of pre-packaged integration modules

- Test: Reading of detailed tuning guides, sample test plans

- Deploy: Reading deployment guides, reading about enterprise subscription or deployment services, and "phone-home" capabilities in the software itself

This framework allowed Terracotta to map and guide the buyer's journey, even in an environment where direct interaction with the end purchaser was quite rare. Sales professionals at Terracotta were provided with deep insights into the buyer stage for each of their accounts, and were sent real-time notifications as buyers progressed from one stage to another.

Over 6 iterations, the Terracotta team continually refined their algorithms for understanding their audience. Insights such as a tight focus on recency and frequency as factors in evaluating any sign of interest came from this iterative refinement process. Evidence of a need for the high scale clustering software that Terracotta provides could be deemed out of date if it was more than a few months old, due to the changing nature of buyer needs. This detailed, automatically-created map of a buyer's journey allowed their sales team to focus on the key prospects who were ready to move forward with a purchase, and allow marketing to guide the evolution of the others.

tion of buying events, the goals you pursue change the measurements you employ.

After you decide the goal you are measuring, compare the raw, non-categorized scores to the results. This affords two opportunities to optimize the scoring: the algorithm itself and the breakpoints at which one process is chosen over another or the lead is handed to sales. With the raw scoring data and the results, it's easier to see the strong correlations between leads that received high scores and resulted in successful sales. High correlations, of course, give the marketer greater confidence in the lead-scoring. If high correlations are absent, it's likely the algorithm needs refinement.

When is a lead good enough to hand over to sales? What is the right break point for choosing one follow-up process (*vs.* another)? When is the ideal point to hand the lead to sales? This is the second optimization point for the lead-scoring model. If there's a strong correlation between lead scores and success, many marketers will actually tweak the break point to optimize the overall process. It might actually be desirable to lower the breakpoint/threshold in order to fill the sales team's funnel (even if the leads are of slightly lower quality). Or it may be more desirable to raise the bar for hand-off to sales so that a smaller team can focus on higher-quality opportunities.

Forrester Research: Lead Scoring on a Content Rich Site

Forrester Research has an extremely active website due to the high value research on the site. The research they provide is read by hundreds of thousands of people. Intermingled in this traffic, however, is a group of qualified prospects for the Forrester research sales team. The job of discovering the qualified prospects among this crowd fell to the Forrester marketing team.

To do this, the marketing and sales teams carefully planned and categorized what would make an ideal prospect. Forrester markets based on 21 profiles of research interest, categorizing their prospect community into interest roles such as CMOs, CIOs, and eBusiness Leaders. Each of these is associated with specific research articles on their website. This information, in combination with company size and industry information, allowed Forrester to reach an agreement with their sales team on the ideal prospect.

The Forrester marketing team queried 50 members of their sales organization—from reps to management to understand what a lead was to them, how they judged them, and what information was most relevant to them. From this, and based on their assessment of the research articles on their website, they built, and gained agreement on, a scoring algorithm that scored prospects uniquely against each interest profile.

The leads were ranked as A, B, C, or D leads. A and B leads were passed to sales, C and D leads were nurtured with offers of research in a carefully constructed program. From this starting point, the sales team was engaged in a quarterly review cycle. Each quarter, the marketing team presented aggregate data on the results (number of A and B leads generated) and engaged sales in detailed discussions on algorithm adjustment. Each proposed adjustment was then used to rescore the entire quarter's leads to understand how the numbers and scores would have worked out had that been the algorithm.

Through working with sales to optimize the process, Forrester was able to learn some critical elements and make adjustments. For example, Forrester built in a "locking" rule to ensure that once a lead was marked as an A or B lead and passed to sales it was not to be rescored for a 90 day period in order to allow sales sufficient time to follow up with it without seeing score changes due to recently viewed content as activity contributed to a score only for a short duration. Similarly, adjustments were made to the relative contribution of company size and industry to ensure that prospects with no ability to purchase were not passed forward regardless of their level of activity.

Continued optimization of the process allows Forrester's sales and marketing teams to continually refine their mutual understanding of a lead, and focus on efforts that best contribute to the flow of high quality leads to sales.

6
SIX

NURTURE TO WIN

Marketers have it backward.

Historically, with complex products and services, most marketers have aspired to lead a prospective buyer through a progression of steps and phases, ultimately resulting in a purchase. Increasingly, that model has no place in today's complex sales. Today, buyers are driven more by internal events inside their own organizations that compel them to initiate and undertake the purchasing process. They're the ones with control – and they have no use for a marketer-defined sales cycle.

Marketers must continually refine their abilities to identify a prospect's stage in the buying cycle and associated buying interest- and ensuring that the prospect receives that corresponding message that is appropriate based on those stages and interest levels. Failure leads to a process mismatch where an "early" prospect can be deemed unqualified and dropped from a sales funnel simply because they were not in an active buying cycle at that moment.

But that lead still has important value. How should marketers handle the "not-quite-ready" leads that may blossom later? The answer is "nurture marketing" – a thoughtful strategy to stay in front of prospects, present relevant messaging that elicits responses, keep the dialogue going, and monitor for changes in buying interest that might signal movement to a next step in the buying process

⇨ GET STARTED NOW

TRADESHOW OR EVENT FOLLOW-UP

Chances are, most people at the typical tradeshow are not ready to buy at that very moment. They are usually earlier in their buying process—self-educating about the market and identifying potentially suitable vendors. A simple three- or five-step automated nurture campaign is a great way to introduce these show leads to your market space and your solution. When they reach an active-buying stage, your lead scoring will alert you.

PHILOSOPHY OF NURTURE MARKETING

Inherently, nurture marketing is not intended to aggressively drive a prospect to take actions. It is merely intended to keep the conversation with the prospect going and continue to deliver a soft-sell, low-key message to a prospect at early stages of the buying process. This accomplishes two things:

- It helps the vendor retain top-of-mind awareness with the prospect and encourages subsequent engagement with the vendor when the prospect advances through the buying process

- It affords numerous opportunities for the prospect to engage with the vendor, each of which leaves a unique digital body language fingerprint that enables the marketer to identify changes in buying status.

Nurture marketing must be directed to *retain the prospect's permission* to stay in front of them. That permission is secured only if the message or communication contains sufficient value to the recipient and encourages him to remain engaged with the vendor.

By "permission," we don't mean the tactical opt-in permission of subscription management that's often associated with aspects of digital marketing. In this context, it refers to a much broader measure of the prospect's engagement with the brand and organization. After all, even tactical opt-in permission doesn't mean much to the marketer if the duly and legitimately subscribed prospect is receiving the marketing messaging but has long since stopped reading it because it offers no value.

THE DIGITAL BODY LANGUAGE OF PERMISSION

Digital body language provides the relevant construct to more effectively understand the prospect's engagement with the brand and whether the vendor retains the prospect's permission to continue to present marketing messages. For instance, with e-mail campaigns, high open-rates, good forwarding rates, repeated opens, and strong click-through rates all indicate strong permission. With direct mail, the use of individually trackable call-to-action items (e.g. campaign-specific 1-800 numbers, promotion codes, or personal URLs) come together to form digital body language to indicate permission.

⇨ *GET STARTED NOW*

NURTURE THE LEAKY FUNNEL

Some sales leads "leak" out of the funnel. They aren't losses. They aren't wins. They're just "quiet" and haven't—after a period of weeks or months—entered an active sales process. Often, these leads are engaged by sales—but before they were ready to begin an active sales process. In many organizations, this is paradoxically one of the best lead sources, so don't let those get away

---

One pitfall: tying the call-to-action too closely to a purchase event. Overtly promotional messaging can reduce a prospect's responsiveness to your messages. With calls to action, it can be a great temptation to use a promotional offer to encourage a purchase. However, if the prospect in the nurturing program is only at the awareness, education, or discovery stages, he will reject a purchase-linked incentive or call-to-action. This doesn't mean he's uninterested—only that he isn't at the stage where he's ready to purchase. Avoid the mistake of writing him off simply because he didn't respond to a purchase-linked call to action.

BUYER SEGMENT NURTURING

Once the marketer has effectively segmented the prospect base according to buyer role, buyer stage, or level of interest, it's possible to target the nurture-marketing messages much more effectively. The degree of message targeting that the marketer chooses to implement likely

> ⇨ *GET STARTED NOW*

CAPTURE POINTS, SALES, AND NURTURING
Every time you capture contact information—such as Web forms, event registrations, and downloads—think of it another opportunity to nurture the prospect with the right information rather than simply handing off to sales. Understand what the prospect is likely seeking at that point in the buying process and provide a path to that information. A direct hand off to sales is only appropriate if the prospect explicitly requests it or if your lead-scoring algorithm indicates the prospect has entered an active buying stage. In the vast majority of contact-capture instances, this is not the case.

depends on the resources that the organization can bring to bear on the challenge.

There are profound implications in the simple change from marketing by a selling process to marketing based on nurturing prospective buyers. The promising luster of one-to-one marketing was tarnished in its early implementations as prospects quickly recognized that they were receiving generic messages—with merely a mail-merged "Dear Firstname" tacked to the beginning. However, with prospect profiling and lead scoring to identify buying cycle segments and interest levels, marketers can now craft and hone messages that are catered to the real needs of the buyer at that moment in time.

NURTURE FEEDERS AND EXITS

The untold truth about marketing today: at any given time, most prospects shouldn't be in the sales funnel. They should be in a nurturing program. If they are not in the nurture program or are in the sales funnel, then, by definition, one should assume that those leads not target buyers or influencers or that permission to present a message to them has been revoked. The challenge, however, is that to effectively segment and manage, marketers must maintain detailed processes for:

- Adding the right people to a nurture campaign.

- Transferring leads from a nurture campaign to an active sales process (at precisely the correct juncture in the sales cycle).

- Moving leads from one nurture sequence to another when the demonstrated or deduced interest area or level changes.

- Purging leads from a nurture campaign or downgrading communication frequency when the marketer has lost permission to present a message to them.

- Removing prospects from communication when it is determined that they are not potential buyers

This is accomplished through nurture feeders and exits. The feeder is a system for automatically defining and

Concur: From Stories to Success—Nurturing an Influencer

Concur's "True Tales of Business Travel" campaign had bridged the gap between awareness and engagement of business travelers through a creative viral campaign (highlighted in Chapter 2). A shift in Concur's focus towards small and medium businesses had meant that the business end-user had a greater influence on the decision to purchase a corporate expense management solution.

To enable this potential influencer to help guide the buying process, however, Concur needed to ensure that they were able to convey the right message about the value of Concur's solutions.

Many of the visitors to the stories site would sign up for a free trial of Concur Expense, and the goal was now to enable these users to influence a purchase decision. To do this, Concur recognized that two parallel activities needed to take place. Firstly, the user had to have a positive, and high-value experience with the product. Secondly, the user needed to be able to convey that value to the ultimate decision makers in the organization.

Throughout the 90-day trial experience, a multi-step nurture campaign provided tips and tricks on getting the most out of the trial service, and focused on adding value to the prospect's day. A parallel message to each tip or trick focused on the broader value a company would get while using Concur's full-service version with the intent of sharing that information within the organization to accounting and finance. Throughout the process, Concur monitored the prospect's digital body language, both in their response to the marketing and in their engagement with the free trial.

At the end of 90 days, the prospect had remained engaged, but had not been aggressively sold to. The Concur sales team was notified with the leads that came from this trial process, and was given insight into what they had found interesting, and what areas of the product had been used. Key metrics like the number of expense reports submitted within the product were used to qualify each prospect for sales follow-up.

collecting prospects based on pre-defined traits observed and classified in digital body language. Once these prospects are collected, they can be inaugurated into a multi-step nurturing program.

At the other end of the nurturing program are exits - the complement to feeders. An exit is an automated way to remove prospects from the nurturing program based on defined, observable events, ranging from voluntarily entering an active sales cycle to signs of disengagement with the messaging of the nurturing program. Since the goal is to maintain permission to keep delivering messages to prospects in the nurture program, it is crucial to read the prospect's digital body language carefully and treble down the frequency and intensity of nurture messages if the prospect begins to show signs of disinterest.

Based on the digital body language observed, marketing might pass a lead to sales. However, that handoff isn't always successful. Sometimes sales rejects the lead despite marketing's lead-scoring analysis. The sales rep might fail to connect with the lead or otherwise take no action. But marketers mustn't let their efforts to cultivate that lead fall by the wayside. That's where clawbacks enter the picture.

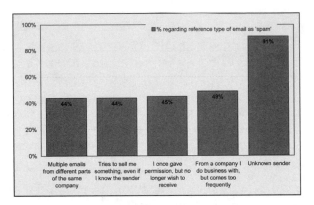

Figure 21: Marketing Sherpa stats show that prospects will view your messaging as spam if they lose interest in your messaging

With a clawback, the marketer revokes a lead that has already been passed to sales. After a defined period of time (e.g. 30 days), if no action is taken, or the lead has not reached a certain status, marketing pulls the lead back into nurture program to ensure that the tailored communications with the prospect continue.

FUNNEL LEAKAGE AND NURTURE MARKETING

By carefully defining, calibrating, and configuring the feeders, exits, and clawbacks, marketers can minimize so-called "funnel-leakage." This deterioration of the sales pipeline occurs as a result of any or all of the following:

- Falsely assuming that a prospective buyer is "ready to close" when, in fact, they are not.

- A failure to communicate the right message at the right time to the right person.

- A failed hand-off to sales.

- A fundamental loss of interest in a solution or solution area.

- Overcommunication leading to disengagement

The only reason for removing a prospect from the overall revenue creation funnel is due to them being the wrong target, or a fundamental loss of interest. The other situations should only lead the marketer to move the prospective buyer up or down the funnel based on the observed digital body language. It should NOT cause them to leak out of the funnel altogether.

NURTURE, TRUST, AND BRAND

Given the dynamics of a complex-sales process, many prospective buyers may remain in various stages of the sales funnel for extended periods of time. During an extended period of nurture marketing, marketers should approach the challenge with a long-term perspective. Marketers can no longer simply devote their efforts to blindly pushing a prospect through a seller-defined sales process. Buyers no longer tolerate that outmoded thinking. Instead, today's marketers must provide appropriate ways to enable buyers to take self-directed actions consistent with their buying interests. The marketer no longer leads. He follows the buyer and observes the digital body language that indicates what activities have taken place.

VOXIFY: REJUVENATING DEAD LEADS THROUGH NURTURING

Voxify is a provider of powerful speech applications for contact centers in retail, travel, hospitality, entertainment, financial services, and healthcare. Its complex sales cycle can often stretch 12-18 months, which makes it a challenge to align sales resources with leads. At one point, more than 3,000 leads sat idle—leads that could potentially buy Voxify's software.

Without a structured follow-up system, Voxify was wasting opportunity. If a lead was not ready to buy at the time of initial contact, the lead was recycled; however there was not a process to ensure further communication. Given the length of the sales cycle, and the type of internal project that would drive the need for Voxify's solutions, this meant that many valid – but early – leads were leaking out of the funnel.

The breadth of Voxify's target markets, combined with the range of possible solutions, meant the company employed a broad matrix of messaging to ensure relevance with the prospect. A matrix of 26 separate industry and education topics was created with each topic adding value to each unique buyer type and stage in the buying process. An automated nurture campaign kept this messaging in front of the "cooler" leads to maintain their interest level and watch for signs of changes to buying behavior as the messaging evolved from "why speech applications" through to "why Voxify".

Within six months, the so-called "cooler" leads became the largest source of conversion for new sales opportunities. The campaign created 1,500 responses and enabled more than 400 companies to re-engage with the sales force. The nurture campaign also allowed the sales team to better understand whether the prospect was more interested in a specific vertical application such as a flight check-in system, or in a horizontal application such as a generic routing agent, and cater their conversation accordingly. By keeping relevant, topical messaging in front of prospective buyers, without overtly selling, Voxify identified and acted on buying interest when it arose.

The goal of nurture marketing is to retain the prospect's permission to continue to deliver messages. That's only possible by continuing to add value and provide content that spurs interest. A nurture program is the ideal forum on which to base thought leadership messaging structures that build credibility, enhance the brand, and establish the vendor as a trusted resource in the mind of the prospect.

REGAINING LOST PERMISSION

As discussed earlier, the importance of maintaining the prospects' permission to remain in front of them with messaging is paramount. But that requires a delicate balance. If you abuse that privilege, perceptions of your company can rapidly shift from "potential partner" to "spammer" regardless of whether the prospect had explicitly signed up to receive communications from you, or indeed whether they select to opt out.

But what should a marketer do when that implicit permission has been lost? At first glance, it can appear to be an unsolvable paradox: after you've lost the prospect's

BELLA PICTURES: DIRECT MAIL IN NURTURE MARKETING

As the premier provider of wedding photography in the United States, Bella Pictures deals with a very defined prospect audience: recently engaged brides-to-be. The sales cycle itself involves an equally well-structured timeframe as anyone who has been involved with the planning of a wedding can attest. To maximize its success, Bella guides brides through photography selection using a carefully crafted nurture program that starts with the first contact with the bride.

One of the key conversion points for brides-to-be was the initial meeting with a photographer to discuss her photographic preferences. In the hectic process of planning a wedding, a meeting with a photographer could easily be forgotten, or the bride could show up without having thought through the questions she would be asked, such as the type of photography, styles, album choices, and special shots to request.

To resolve this challenge in the process, Bella Pictures turned to direct mail. A postcard was sent to each bride, targeted to arrive just days before her scheduled meeting date. The direct-mail piece served three purposes. First, it reminded the bride of her upcoming meeting with her photographer. Second, it presents a tangible, high-quality piece to the bride to impress on the bride the aspects of photographic quality that are likely to be important. And third, the direct-mail piece provided a checklist for the bride to work from, ensuring that she had considered all the key photography decisions she would have to make.

In a sequence timed around the bride's wedding date, the nurture process guides the bride through the timelines and decisions needed. By orienting its marketing process around the bride and her decision process, Bella significantly lifts its conversion rate from initial contact to booked appointments. Even with direct mail, which is typically not viewed as a drip/nurture marketing vehicle, Bella aligns with the bride's buying process.

attention by communicating incorrectly, what communication-oriented strategy regains that lost permission if it cannot, by definition, reach the prospect?

Naturally, the first step is to identify these wayward prospects. Again, digital body language plays the lead role here because loss of interest and marketing disengagement typically embodies a clear pattern. We've all seen the physical examples in meetings: yawning, checking a Blackberry, or looking around the room (or out the window). Just as these clearly communicate (sometimes painfully) a prospect's disinterest in a conference room, digital body language can also betray disinterest. The easiest to spot, of course, is a pattern of zero activity in response to regular and frequent communication. For instance, a prospective buyer who receives regular e-mail messages but who does not open them multiple times, does not forward any of them, does not click on any of the links in the e-mail, and engages in no events has almost certainly disengaged from the marketing messaging.

There's a key pitfall that many marketers fall into after they identify their inactive buyers: they immediately seek to re-engage before they understand why the disengagement occurred. Poorly targeted messaging, inappropri-

VFA: NURTURING TO RE-ENGAGE DEAD LEADS

VFA, a leading provider of end-to-end solutions for facilities capital planning and asset management, had many dormant leads in its marketing database. Amassed over a period of years, through tradeshows, lists and sales activities, these "dead" leads were stored in VFA's CRM system, had never been converted to opportunities, and were no longer receiving communications from VFA.

To engage these leads, VFA implemented a 5-part nurturing program that provided unique content to each of the 6 verticals targeted by VFA. The initial communications were case study focused, and progressed to white paper and webinar downloads, then offers to request a demo or engage directly with sales.

At each step of the process VFA's marketing team enabled the prospect to engage in a way that was governed by the prospect's own buying process. Each email offer connected to a landing page that described how similar organizations were able to meet their business challenges. Additional resources—articles, case studies, white papers—were offered, allowing prospects to select the information they needed depending on their stage in the buying process. At each step, the prospect had the ability to "short cut" the process and jump straight to a later stage; by either requesting a demo or engaging with the VFA sales team.

The campaign succeeded in bringing back a tremendous number of leads from the "dead". Over 120 highly qualified leads were passed to sales, and over $1.6M in pipeline was created. In a typical example, a lead may have been disqualified at a much earlier date, but given changes in the prospect's organization, they were now ready to purchase and a sales opportunity was discovered. Only through nurturing and observing the buyers' digital body language were these opportunities rediscovered.

ate segmentation, or low-value content can be culprits to look for. Simply going back with the same messaging and frequency is to repeat the same mistakes—a recipe for failure and frustration for both buyer and seller.

Many marketers find that it is worth the investment to seek out and directly engage with a sample of prospects (perhaps in a focus-group forum) to better understand this disengagement. If disengagement is happening in a broad manner across your prospect base, it may be the sign of some significant messaging challenges.

Once the marketer discovers and remedies the factors that led to disengagement, the challenge is crafting a relevant and appropriate way to re-engage the prospect. Since they are, by definition, disengaged, this is no small challenge.

One of the most common—and successful—approaches is to reengage the fallen-away prospect using a media type that is very different from the primary media type that the prospect is accustomed to receiving from the vendor. In many instances, the prospect's disengagement is inherently tied to the media type on which they typically see your messages. For example, if you send a weekly e-mail, the prospect can soon grow to reflexively delete your message, sight unseen. If you try to re-engage them with the same media type (*i.e.,* another e-mail), the chances are high that the effort will once again meet a reflexive deletion before it's even opened. By re-engaging on an unexpected media type, you may receive

FORRESTER RESEARCH: REACTIVATION CAMPAIGN PRIOR TO A DATABASE CLEANSE

Forrester Research is a very well known leader of the analyst space, and has been so for many years. As such, they had been able to develop a large database of prospect names over the years. However, as with many large databases of prospects, a segment of this database was totally inactive. No marketing had been done to these prospects for at least a year, and no activity had been seen from them in a comparable amount of time.

Forrester was interested in cleansing their marketing database in order to remove data on prospects for whom there was no interest, but prior to doing this, they decided to launch a campaign to attempt to revive this segment of the database and share with them the major improvements in the Forrester web experience that had happened over the year. If they were unable to revive the prospects' interest, they would be removed from the database.

Forrester markets based on 21 explicit, self-selected roles. For the inactive segment of their database, they targeted an offer of free research at the prospects based on this role, or based on selecting a role for those who had not yet self-selected. The landing page offered research that was related to other research profiles in case interests or roles had changed in the time that had passed.

A two-part campaign of email and direct mail (with personal URLs) was used to engage with the list. Forrester then watched the prospects' activity to understand if there was interest or engagement. Those who took an action, such as downloading the research were deemed reactivated. Those who did not were cleansed from the database.

> The reactivation campaign was a great success for Forrester and flooded their website with traffic. By understanding the digital body language of these prospects, Forrester was able to understand who had gone quiet, and what it would take to reengage with them. Out of this campaign, from prospects who were due to be deleted from the database, significant revenue pipeline was created.

a chance to re-engage the prospect. Voice or direct mail can be very effective for these purposes.

Marketers must make sure that the content re-engagement campaigns are sufficiently interesting or valuable to recapture their interest. It might even be wise to acknowledge the disengagement upfront (e.g. "We haven't heard from you recently...") before proceeding. You may only have a single opportunity to re-engage, so it's critical to ensure you are delivering sufficient value in your message. The goal is to make the prospect glad that he took the time to read your message in that re-engagement communication.

CAMPAIGN PLANNING

In this new marketing environment, timing is everything. Think of your marketing communications process as a series of stages. When a potential buyer is nothing more than a "suspect," he must first be engaged. But if he's close to a purchase, he needs a buyer's kit of evaluation tools. If you time those messages out of sequence, you cannot effectively market to that prospect. While every business and market is different (and you should spend careful time analyzing what campaigns are appropriate for the various stages of your prospect's buying cycle), some of the different campaigns can include:

Awareness

- Inactive re-engagement
- Competitive-loss re-engagement
- Thought leadership newsletter
- "Net-New" contact welcome program

Discovery

- Search campaign—broad terminology
- Advertising (banner, etc)
- Tradeshow presence

Validation

- Interest conversion
- Evaluator education
- Objection campaign
- Buyer's kit (ROI tools, case studies, demos)

Post-Sale

- Customer follow-up
- Customer loyalty and retention
- Customer renewal

SEVEN

THE EMERGING
NEW DISCIPLINE

Marketers *can* succeed in today's transformed buying environment by adapting their thinking and embracing the new realities of marketing to online buyers. But that doesn't mean the adaptation is simple. On the contrary—it requires the entire organization to make significant changes to marketing. Previously, marketers emphasized creative images, clever concepts, and careful wording. While those valuable disciplines still play a role, increasingly, they're taking a back seat to the ability to understand and respond to the nuances of digital body language that appear in prospective buyers' online behaviors and activities.

THE NEW THOUGHT PROCESS

Forward-thinking demand-generation marketers are adopting entirely new perspectives on how they engage with prospects. They're bringing digital body language off the whiteboard and into the market to achieve new levels of effectiveness in sales and marketing. The paradigm is centered on four key principles:

- Digital body language everywhere
- Communications to segments
- Marketing as a process ecosystem
- Data management

⇨ *GET STARTED NOW*

MARKETING ASSETS AND WEB FORMS

The easiest way to get started with leveraging your marketing data and getting to know your prospects better is to place a brief Web form in front of your marketing assets. Don't try to capture all possible information—just a bare minimum (or else you may discourage the visitor from continuing the process). With the right info-capture form, you're better positioned to understand who your prospects are and how they're interacting with your marketing messages.

DIGITAL BODY LANGUAGE EVERYWHERE

The first step in leveraging digital body language is simply to ensure that it is efficiently and completely captured at all appropriate touchpoints that a prospect has with the organization. Each interaction must be carefully considered for the insights it can provide and how the information is captured.

Next, it's important to link the data to other sources of insight and data. At that particular point in time, or with that specific marketing asset, it may not be possible to uniquely know which prospect is interacting with the organization. However, it may very well be possible to correlate interactions from multiple prospects with other information that is known about them. For example, examine the search terms that visitors use to reach the corporate Web site and analyze their navigation of your site.

⇨ *GET STARTED NOW*

GATED FORMS AND
PROGRESSIVE DISCLOSURE

Web forms should create a series of appropriate low-hurdle gates to your marketing assets. Think of each one as an equitable exchange of information. At each step, ask for an incremental amount of information. Ensure you can pre-populate your Web forms based on the visitor's cookie, and pre-sent fields in that form based on what information has already been requested. Elegant execution provides a seamless experience for the visitor who is never asked more than two or three questions. Yet, that progressive disclosure provides richer insight and understanding.

Over time and, perhaps, with multiple interactions, the prospect profile builds. Soon, it may be possible to link unique sequences of site activities to a known individual. From here, the prospect profile can be built to enhance the knowledge of that individual's digital body language.

A variety of techniques are applicable, and successful demand-generation marketers always work to ensure that touchpoints are comprehensively monitored. Even typically offline media, such as direct mail, can provide significant insights into interest levels of individual prospects if they use a personal URL (www.acme.com/johnsmith) for each recipient as their unique call-to-action.

There's also a healthy variety in the way marketers capture prospect information. Rigorously analyze each marketing touchpoint and determine precisely what it can potentially indicate about a prospect's propensity to purchase.

Think about the depth and breadth of the information that can be captured. Information depth provides more compelling insights into a buyer's area or level of interest. You can analyze which exact search terms were used on Google, for instance. Or you can record which sequence of screens within a Flash demo that were actually viewed. These data points offer significantly more insight than the mere fact that the visitor was referred by Google or viewed the Flash demo.

In addition, marketers should always rely on breadth of insight as an important component of their philosophy and approach in structuring marketing campaigns. For example, a content feed of related-content items in a Web site sidebar or in outgoing e-mails, can be a valuable technique for broadening insight. A prospect who clicks on a related-content item has disclosed that he may have an interest that is close to what was originally understood, but broader in terms of topics of interest.

COMMUNICATION TO SEGMENTS

It's a good idea to view outbound campaigns in a whole new light: by examining the segments of buyers that marketers can define using digital body language. A webinar may focus on thought leadership or awareness in the market space and therefore target prospects early in the buying process. There may also be an aspect of classical segment-based marketing where one targets only pharmaceutical companies in Western Europe. But most importantly, the marketer must think about seg-

➡ *GET STARTED NOW*

ACTIVITY PROFILING:
UNDERSTANDING YOUR DATA

Activity measurements are an incredibly useful metric for marketers. How often are you communicating with each prospect? Are those prospects "active"—that is, are they opening e-mails, visiting your site, and downloading your white papers? Explore your data to get this high-level view and look for opportunities to either target the "quiet corners" of your database or reduce your frequency to over-communicated prospects.

---

ments that are defined by the stage of the buying process as presented by the buyer's digital body language.

To achieve this effectively, a new level of operational discipline in marketing is essential. First, we must examine the data model. Earlier, we discussed how the rich profiling information that marketers collect sheds meaningful light on a buyer's mindset. But for that information to be useful, it must be aggregated in scoring systems that help marketers understand and define where the buyer is in the process—and what type of communication they would most welcome.

To support communication to these segments, the marketing data model must reflect this. Historically, data models have collected information such as name, contact details, company, industry, and revenue range, but now's the time to vastly expand this thinking. To allow a field marketer to properly and appropriately invite early-stage prospects to a webinar, the underlying data model must enable the marketer to understand the prospect's buying stage. Similarly, if one only wanted to invite evaluators and technical buyers, it's important to first be able to define in the data model the information that will reflect this.

Supported by a very solid data model, demand-generation marketers must think about the transitions that buyers make between buying-cycle stages. If the prospect has been in a long-term nurturing campaign but is now starting to show significant interest, what is the right action plan? If a lead is handed off to sales, should the marketer continue or suspend efforts to market to that lead? If the salesperson meets a prospect and adds him to a sales campaign for product A based on their conversation, should the prospect be removed from campaigns discussing product B?

All of these choices and permutations require the savvy demand-generation marketer to work diligently to understand, evaluate, challenge, and configure the surrounding/underpinning processes and flows that enable it all to happen. These processes can evolve slowly and incrementally as the marketing department transitions to a new way of marketing.

The key, however, is that this approach to thinking is not one with which many marketers are familiar. A new discipline in marketing is required to help marketers look beyond yesterday's processes and flows and build new fundamental building blocks of communication with prospects.

CENTRALIZE YOUR DATA

To gain the insights into your prospects' digital body language that you need to succeed, you need to centralize your data. Use the e-mail address as a basis of identification—it is the most common method for communication and is the simplest and cleanest way to build a central marketing data-base from which to communicate and observe digital body language.

DOES SEGMENTATION MATTER?

In a word: *absolutely*. With segmentation, you can focus on the specific metrics and buyer characteristics and provide relevant and timely communication and resources. The following table—from Marketing Sherpa Metrics—shows just how powerful segmentation is.

Marketing as a Process Ecosystem

As we've noted, the transition of marketing from monolithic outbound campaigns governed and catering to the vendor's selling process to new-breed reactive campaigns focused on the prospect's buying process requires no small change in thinking. It requires a marketing team prepared to implement numerous processes that deliver the right communication at the right time to the right prospect.

In that spirit and in pursuit of those goals, demand-generation marketers must carefully contemplate and

PROMOTIONAL EMAIL CAMPAIGNS				
Audience Size	Segmented		Not Segmented	
	Opens	Clicks	Opens	Clicks
< 5K	50.5%	11.70%	5.60%	0.60%
5K–10K	48.80%	9.00%	3.90%	.30%
10K–50K	28.50%	7.60%	4.00%	.50%
50K–100K	13.40%	4.00%	3.70%	0.80%
> 100K	13.10%	1.10%	3.50%	0.20%
Averages	30.86%	6.68%	4.14%	0.48%

coordinate four primary types of automation programs. Each program has unique needs for timing and orchestration with other programs. Together, they form the marketing ecosystem that enables marketers to achieve their ultimate goal: the right message at the right time to the right prospect.

1. Event-Triggered Automation

Perhaps the most common and intuitive way to deliver messaging that is appropriate to a buyer's timeline is through event-triggered automation. This technique uses a (typically prospect-initiated) "event"—such as registering for a webinar, downloading a white paper, or initiating a free-trial—as the starting point for a marketing campaign. All subsequent communications to that individual prospect key off of that start point. For in-

⇨ *GET STARTED NOW*

INBOUND DATA: STANDARD
DATA OPERATIONS

Data has many entry points into your marketing database: Web forms, lists, event attendees, and more. To use these optimally, make certain that the inbound data is clean and consistent. Implement basic data "hygiene" standards through a program that automatically scans and validates every incoming record—whether it's a list or a form. This program can trap duplicates, ensure standardized data values (e.g. "VA" vs. Va. vs. "Virginia") and other data cleansing. With clean, standardized data, your marketing processes and analytics will be significantly simpler, accurate, and cleaner.

stance, the prospect receives a 30-day e-mail precisely 30 days after he first engaged through the initiating event.

In modern marketing organizations, event-triggered marketing is a prevalent and popular way for choreographing prospect communications. After any event that captures prospect interest—either in a continuous fashion (e.g. a whitepaper download) or a repetitive fashion (e.g. a series of tradeshows)—an event-driven communication plan is executed to ensure that the sales message remains top of mind with the prospect.

Tradeshows, white paper downloads, and many similar sources of information are often used early in the buying cycle when buyers seek to gather as much information and solution options as possible to analyze and explore. These events make ideal triggers to start a communication campaign over 60 or 90 days.

2) Marketing-Initiated Programs

Although the use of large-scale outbound campaigns has rightly decreased in many marketing organizations, they nonetheless remain useful in some situations. If an event or news item is driven by a fixed date, large-scale outbound campaigning can drive prospect interest. For example, an upcoming seminar series might require extensive promotion to build attendance. Targeting the right mix of prospects requires careful consideration of their stage in the sales process or area of interest.

However, the transition to a marketing style that embraces the principles of digital body language means that these outbound campaigns should also leverage feeders and exits to move prospects into and out of the outbound campaigns based on whether they can be qualified for a handoff to sales, or if they've been included in other campaigns. Outbound marketing also improves immensely when the tone, style, and content of messaging are carefully calibrated using knowledge of prospects' digital body language

3) Sales-Triggered Campaigns

Sales, of course, is fully capable of initiating and developing relationships with prospects, often adding them to marketing's ongoing nurture campaigns to build on or expand the relationship. This style of campaigning and relationship-development can be extremely effective because it uses the native intuition of the sales professional:

> ⇨ *GET STARTED NOW*

SYNCHRONIZE MARKETING AND SALES DATA
Marketing and sales communicate with the same people—but they may end up with data that doesn't match up. Ensure your marketing and sales data is bi-directionally synchronized. That means eliminating offline lists and multiple independent databases. In many organizations, marketing maintains the superset of data and only hands off records to sales when they are clean, non-duplicated, and qualified.

---

no one knows more about where these prospects are in the sales processes. At the same time, these campaigns support a series of better-targeted communications aimed at moving the prospect to the next stage of the buying process.

Clearly, these processes require a sophisticated level of automation. Sales will continuously add limited numbers of prospects to nurture campaigns, so the communications must be well-timed to align with when the prospect was added.

4) SYSTEM PROCESSES

While this outbound campaigning takes place, demand-generation marketers use background processes across the marketing database to uncover insights, perform key actions, and make various decisions. Simultaneously, these processes can examine a lead's score, determine what buying stage a lead is in, assess their area of interest, route qualified leads to the right salesperson, feed less-qualified leads into nurture campaigns, update and manage data, or clawback leads that have gone dormant with sales reps.

These processes operate continuously behind the scenes, and are instrumental in ensuring a constant flow of the right data between marketing processes. However, as these processes scale up to meet the needs of larger organizations, marketers must adopt an operational mindset like those of many other disciplines such as manufacturing or supply-chain management. Conceptualizing, diagramming, and designing these data-process flows, identifying and handling exceptions, and triggering the handoffs are all new skills for the demand-generation marketer.

DATA MANAGEMENT

Our new marketing discipline is creating a variety of impacts. First, we see a new need to view marketing as an ecosystem of processes. Next, we must make intelligent decisions based on the wealth of data now available to marketing. In turn, this leads to a requirement for greater awareness of the importance of data management in the marketing profession.

Before digital body language emerged as a key foundation for contemporary marketing, monolithic outbound

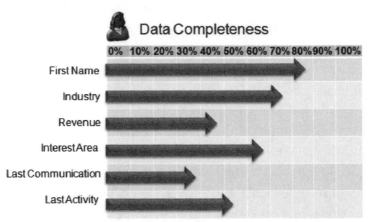

Figure 22: Understanding data completeness is key to marketing success.

campaigns were often fed by a single, purpose-driven list that was typically used for only one campaign—or at most, a very small number of campaigns. Now, to capitalize on digital body language, marketers are working with an *aggregated* view of each prospect that slowly grows and builds on the insights gleaned from many previous campaigns and interactions

That requires a renewed emphasis in marketing on maintaining data quality throughout the lifecycle of the sales lead. There are a number of key aspects to data management that must be taken into account:

1. DATA PROFILING

Data management starts with an exceptionally clear understanding of what data is available and what the quality of that data is. Since marketers generally work

⇨ *GET STARTED NOW*

LEVERAGE EXTERNAL DATA SOURCES

A rich variety of external data sources can provide you with a wealth of insights into each of your prospects—without requiring you to ask them directly. For example, you can often fill in gaps about the prospect's company—such as revenue, industry, employee size, or address—through external sources. By automating this process, you can quickly gain insight and improve marketing effectiveness without burdening your prospect and presenting hurdles.

---

with lists of significant size, the data must be profiled in an aggregate form.

Marketers must first understand their *data completeness*. Which fields in the data model are essential and how complete is the data in those fields? For instance, as marketers create broader and richer profiles on prospects, many data fields will be sparse until the data is captured in the latter stages of the sales cycle. By understanding what data is available and how large a percentage of the database is populated, marketers can design campaigns that either support higher levels of personalization or collect key data elements.

The need to understand data completeness also relates to how a lead has been scored: the stage of the buying process, the area of interest, the level of interest, or communication preference. Without complete data for these fields, it is difficult to target campaigns or personalization using their digital body language.

NATIONAL INSTRUMENTS: MULTIPLE ACTIVITIES LEADING TO MULTIPLE RESPONSES

National Instruments leveraged the rich information on prospects' interests that it gleaned from prospect digital body language on its Web site to deliver highly targeted and relevant communications. The success of these communications was evident in the very high open and click-through rates discussed earlier. To achieve this, however, National Instruments had to overcome an operational challenge.

The mapping of online activities to communications was straightforward, but also created a challenge. What should happen if a site visitor performs multiple actions that warrant a communication? For instance, downloading four whitepapers should not result in four communications.

To ensure that prospects are not inundated if they perform a number of triggering activities, National Instruments built a waiting period of 24 hours into its scoring. If multiple actions were seen in a 24-hour period, the actions were scored individually and the most relevant communication was selected. Similarly, if an action had been performed before (for example, downloading an automated test guide), the prospect was not sent communications that had this as a call to action.

This solved the challenge of too many communications, but National Instruments also realized that certain key actions should bypass this logic. For example, if a visitor abandons a shopping cart, or saves the configuration of a product, a communication would be immediately triggered. The 24-hour delay was reserved for communications that were deemed less critical.

Since National Instruments is a global organization, each time it learned a better way to interact with customers and built processes for doing so, it replicated that logic and structure and separated it from the content. In this manner, it only needed to translate content and messaging to roll out its program to any of 35 countries.

Data consistency is another important element to analyze in profiling the data. As marketing increasingly relies on a base of rules and processes governing its data, such as rules for lead scoring, that data must maintain a high level of consistency to achieve reliable and repeatable marketing processes. For instance, it's easy to read and parse the following list of executive titles and intuitively recognize that they all represent the same title. However, unless *every* record uses the exact same convention for specifying a title, it will be cumbersome (at best) to build rules that leverage this data.

Title
VP Marketing
V.P. Marketing
VP of Marketing
Marketing VP
Vice Pres Marketing
Vice President, Marketing

Figure 23: Data consistency in job titles.

The third key aspect of data profiling is *data quality*. Since data comprises the foundation for contemporary marketing efforts, its quality is a crucial factor in successful execution. Unfortunately, while campaign execution and analysis are predicated on the assumption that all data is equal in quality, this is rarely the case. Virtually every marketing database contains records that are unusable: junk data typed in on a form, records that are invalid (because of bounce-back e-mail addresses or bad postal addresses), duplicate records, or outdated contact information. The presence of poor-quality data reduces the cost-effectiveness of marketing campaigns and diminishes the impact of the messages.

Issues with data quality affect both the explicit data (data that is known about the prospect, such as role and contact information) and implicit data (data that is based on the prospect's actions and responses to marketing). Unresolved, they cause significant variations in the success of any marketing initiatives.

Data-quality remediation should start with addressing any duplication issues by eliminating multiple records for the same individual—so called "de-duping." In addition, marketers must clean and consolidate their explicit data through standard industry tools such as address validation. However, in some cases, the only way to assess the accuracy of information is to analyze its source. For example, in many industries (e.g. retail), the average employee tenure is as low as two years, leading to a steady challenge of inaccurate data based on its poor recency. A marketer must profile the age of the data, both in terms of sourcing and modification, to gain a good perspective on its accuracy.

2. DATA CLEANSING

Once a demand-generation marketer understands the current state of data in the marketing database, it's time to improve the overall quality of the database. Depending on the weaknesses in the data that have been identified and the goals of the marketer, these data-cleansing activities can take many forms.

Figure 24: Data cleansing—both existing data and flows of data into the marketing database must be handled.

Two main aspects must be considered: current data and the flow of new data into the system. Absent a thoughtful consideration of both of these aspects, a marketer can end up with either of two problems. The database can undergo a one-time cleansing but immediately begins to subsequently deteriorate as substandard data resumes its flow into the database. Or marketers can devise a tight process that adds high-quality contact data into a database that is polluted with poor-quality data.

Duplicates are handled in a manner that is largely similar to other areas of data management. One special consideration is that many aspects of digital body language relate to data linked to the individual, but not part of the actual record. For example, a user's activity on the corporate Web site, their response to e-mail communications, and their searches on Google are all highly relevant in understanding their digital body language. If two records in the marketing database belong to the same individual, the marketer must ensure that the data in all of the duplicates is unified into a single record so that the full digital body language is maintained.

Figure 25: Modular profiles maximize available data while minimizing burden on the prospect.

De-duping a marketing database enables marketers to significantly increase their ability to understand and leverage prospects' digital body language. However, its usefulness is significantly limited unless efforts are made to maintain that non-duplicated database over time. Whether it's forms submitted on a Web site, list purchases, event registrations, or contacts flowing in from CRM systems, marketing manages a continuous flow of data into the marketing database.

It's essential to ensure that the team follows structured processes to ensure that this data is clean and de-duplicated *as* it flows into the marketing database. There's nothing more frustrating or pointless than cleansing a database—only to continue to re-create the problem on an ongoing basis.

The actual entries within the records must also be cleansed, standardized, and enhanced. It's a good idea to standardize data elements such as titles, country names, and states and take advantage of opportunities to en-

FLYERS: RENEWAL MARKETING LEADS TO DEEPER INTEREST PROFILING

The Philadelphia Flyers wanted deeper relationships with fans while also driving the highest possible rates of renewal for season-ticket holders. With careful planning, they were able to achieve both of these goals at once.

The team created personal URLs (PURLs) for each season ticket holder (such as http://www.myflyerstickets.com/johnsmith) and invited each customer to his/her personal site to complete the renewal process. On the personal page, personalized content and offers enticed the ticket holder to renew. But just as importantly, the Flyers began to build the basis for a direct online relationship with each fan.

The Flyers's site contains rich information (including video) on players, stats, schedules, and the draft, and through the direct relationship with each season ticket holder that they have now built, the Flyers better understand each fan. By observing each customer's unique digital body language as they look at stats, read up on players, and watch highlights, the Flyers can identify things such as favorite players and whether they prefer stats or highlight reel footage.

In upcoming seasons, the Flyers plan to leverage this rich base of knowledge based on the fans' digital body language to continually strengthen and hone the message. Personalized video and audio messages from each fan's favorite player and RSS feeds of stats and highlights tailored will deepen the team bond.

The Flyers increased online season-ticket renewals from 1% the previous year to 18%. Renewing online also allowed real-time processing so these numbers were available immediately to senior management opposed to the time lag that occurs with processing renewals manually. Of course, the Flyers were also able to deepen their understanding of their fan base and strengthen those relationships significantly.

D&B: DIGITAL BODY LANGUAGE THROUGHOUT CUSTOMER LIFECYCLE

D&B (Dun & Bradstreet) Canada, given their leadership position in business and credit information, wanted to focus on the end of year renewals for their customer base. With significant existing market share, renewal and retention was just as important to them as new customer acquisition.

The initial project they undertook to achieve this goal was focused directly on the renewal period. A progression of emails, triggered by an upcoming renewal date, was sent to the customer at 90, 60, and 30 days prior to renewal. Over the progression of communications, the tone would become increasingly clear in order to encourage the renewal process.

Watching the results, the D&B team noticed two trends. The first was that the customer response to the emails increased as the renewal date approached. Early communications had open rates of 33%, but as the renewal date approached, these rates would jump to 40% showing a significant uptick in interest.

The second trend noticed was a correlation between the renewal interest and direct usage of the D&B service. Adoption was a critical driver of renewal regardless of product line or industry. To continue to grow their adoption rates, D&B then turned to understanding the digital body language of their customers as expressed in their usage of the service. The service was well instrumented, and provided excellent marketing insight into overall usage and feature specific usage patterns for each user.

Conceptually, the team split the customer's first 12 months of their lifecycle into 3 phases, adoption, usage, and renewal. With the renewal phase now fully automated, the marketing team is now focused on the other two phases.

Leveraging their understanding of the prospect's actual system usage, combined with their insight into the relationship between usage and renewal, a series of onboarding communications will ensure every new customer is quickly and seamlessly able to derive value from the service, while a series of tips and tricks emails will then work from an understanding of what features are and are not being used to suggest areas in which a customer can see even more value from the service.

By taking their understanding of digital body language beyond marketing and into the customer lifecycle, D&B is focused on ensuring that their customers' renewal decision is based on a year of maximum success with their service.

sure data cleanliness and consistency on inbound flows. For instance, ensure that all Web forms follow standard patterns—such as using a pick list of three-letter country codes.

With other fields, data-quality efforts require additional effort. Address fields, for example, may require the marketer to leverage specialized data services to ensure that any given prospect's address is correct and standardized for his geography. Applying these data services to all marketing data—both for the one-time cleanup of the main database and on an ongoing basis with inbound data flows—is the responsibility of the demand-generation marketer.

Marketers may also seek to apply data-management disciplines for other purposes. It's well known, of course, that the more information you request from a prospect

76ERS: MULTI-CHANNEL CAMPAIGN TO WIN BACK SEASON TICKET HOLDERS

The purchase of season tickets for the Philadelphia 76ers is a purchase decision driven by the excitement and emotion that a basketball team brings its fans. It is also a purchase decision that involves a significant financial outlay, however, so the 76ers marketing team needed to ensure that they made the right emotional connections as they communicated with their audience.

A campaign to reconnect with past season ticket holders who had not renewed was initiated. A multi-channel campaign brought the excitement of the basketball experience to the target audience. First, a direct mail piece and a postcard were sent, inviting the recipients to a Select-A-Seat event. A follow-up email campaign shared the creative of the direct mail pieces, and both media types provided a personal URL (PURL) to each recipient that provided highly personalized content and introduced the recipient to their sales representative.

An outbound IVR-based phone campaign recorded by the 76ers president and general manager Ed Stefanski again invited recipients to the Select-A-Seat campaign. At each step, an option to jump straight to purchasing tickets was provided, and for those who showed interest by interacting with the marketing campaign, but either did not attend or did not purchase, the sales team followed up with directly.

The campaign was a great success, with numerous people rejoining the Sixers family as season ticket holders. The resulting revenue generated was more than 35 times the cost of the campaign. By using a variety of media types to bring the emotional experience of basketball into a marketing campaign, the 76ers were able to better connect with their audience.

on a form, the less likely he is to complete and submit it. A demand-generation marketer who invests in appropriate data-quality tools and services can use them to his advantage in this situation.

For instance, once the site visitor provides a company name, it's easier to discover the revenue and industry information. With a postal code or zip code, some address information can be populated. The goal is to reduce, simplify, or auto-populate fields to increase the "fill rate"—the rate at which prospects fill out forms. This is particularly crucial at the early stages of the buying process because it better enables the marketer to capture more data relating to the digital body language of the prospect.

3. Data Operations

Of course, this accurate, up-to-date, and clean data is only useful if the marketer can effectively leverage it to optimize his understanding or communication with prospects. That crucial decoding task falls to the demand-generation marketer. That requires the ability to pass that rich, clean, and complete prospect data to systems and databases that enable the creation of lists, processes, feeders, and segments—to see the digital body language. As the marketing organization evolves in its sophistication and use of digital body language cues, it will experience new pressures to maintain a well-structured environment for exploring and using the richness of this information.

To design a data model for gathering, storing, and maintaining information on prospects, first consider how that data will be used. The goal is to create a database that is relatively simple enough to let the broader marketing team select segments of prospective buyers based on the key metrics of their digital body language. The marketer must consider how the combination of explicit data (contact information), implicit data (activity and response information), and lead scores are stored and leveraged to define market segments.

Ensuring that the right data is available in the right structure to enable the automation of processes and communications to targeted buyer segments requires a sophisticated understanding of data management and information technology—skills that, today, are atypical for many marketing organizations.

By delivering a better understanding of prospects, this new discipline within marketing departments can increase the overall effectiveness of efforts to identify and cultivate qualified buying opportunities. Without a dramatic realignment of marketing to become an operational, process-oriented, data-driven discipline, the opportunities to better engage with prospects remain theoretical. At the core of this shift is the emergence of the demand-generation marketer.

BELLA PICTURES: DATA MANAGEMENT THROUGHOUT A CUSTOMER LIFECYCLE

Brides-to-be purchasing wedding photography services from Bella Pictures are, like brides everywhere, juggling millions of details concerning their big day. To maximize its customer volume in a referral-based industry, Bella was intensely committed to ensuring a pleasant, stress-free buying experience for its customers.

This required operational excellence in the marketing organization. Each communication to brides was carefully designed and monitored by marketing to create a seamless, rewarding experience. That meant the data modeling—even on a concept as simple as an engaged couple—became quite complex. First, Bella modeled the couple just like you would for many marketing organizations. The bride, groom, in-laws, and aunts were each modeled as contacts associated with the couple. From there, the couple had a product selection—multiple photography packages and multiple payment options—associated with their account.

The milestones in the wedding process (location selected, wedding complete, digital negatives signed off, photo album selected) and the details of payment were recorded in detail. Against this data model, Bella built numerous marketing rules to ensure that the bride never received any incorrect or poorly timed communications that would create unnecessary stress.

For each communication, Bella performed a real-time check against the data to ensure the bride was not asked to complete something she had previously provided. Any communication about money was governed by a rule to ensure the bride was never asked about money beneath a certain minimum threshold. By ensuring a very smooth end-to-end process, Bella keeps brides extremely happy, driving significant new business through referrals from satisfied customers.

EIGHT

A NEW COLLABORATIVE MODEL

It's no secret: sales and marketing have never enjoyed the smoothest of relationships—especially in complex-sales environments. Sales representatives complain that the leads they receive from marketing are not of high enough quality and not worth the time required to follow up. Meanwhile, marketers gripe about the frustration of generating what they consider high-quality leads that the sales team ignores.

The roots of this conflict lie in an inherent misalignment of goals, metrics, and motivations—and, most importantly, divergent perspectives of lead quality. This dynamic tension is understandable, given how marketing traditionally operated. Typical contact information about a prospect revealed almost nothing meaningful about the prospect's buying process, role, or interest. It's not too difficult to see how sales might find that many were, indeed, unqualified.

To pass this hurdle, marketers began to ask a series of qualification questions about their budget, purchasing authority, need, purchase timeframe, and other key data. Even this, however, fell well short of what sales needed because the fact is, most prospects routinely answered these questions in a less-than-forthcoming manner that didn't reflect the internal dynamics of their organizations.

Digital body language can improve the alignment of sales and marketing by presenting a common under-

⇨ *GET STARTED NOW*

UNKNOWN VISITOR FOLLOW UP

Many people visit your site each day. Some are driven there by referrals from other sites. Some arrive by searching. Others simply type your Web URL directly into their browser. You may not know much about your visitor, but you can deduce a few things. First, this is a prospect who is at least deep enough in his buying process that he is seeking information on solutions and vendors. Second, you may also be able to tell what company this person is visiting from. Just these two pieces of information indicate that a buying event may be happening at that company. A call to that organization may give you a chance to get involved in a buying process that competitors don't know about.

---

standing of the challenges of revenue generation, and a common set of metrics and goals to work toward.

A COMMON CURRENCY

Sales and marketing can align their objectives by jointly agreeing on the right criteria, metrics, and weights to use in scoring leads. For marketing, the challenge is to generate and cultivate a certain number of leads that meet jointly defined qualification levels. For sales, the task is to ensure these leads turn into revenue.

By understanding what it takes to cultivate leads until they reach specific qualification levels and their subsequent likelihood of closing, marketing, sales, and finance can jointly decide how to allocate their resources, funding, and effort to optimize revenue and meet business goals. Without this common currency—the objectively scored lead—this collaboration is not possible. Instead, the participants will remain persistently mired in their conflicts and never achieve the ability to rise above their differences.

To begin, let's look at the common terms for potential buyers as they move through a buying process. At each step, marketing or sales defines the criteria that must be present (and in sufficient quantity) to confidently conclude that the prospective buyer is far enough along in the buying process to warrant further attention or specific actions. Sirius Decisions, an analyst group who studies the relationship between sales and marketing, has produced a framework for the hand-off of a qualified lead that captures the essence of the process very well:

- **Inquiry**—The prospect takes explicit action such as submitting a form, downloading a trial, or registering for an event.

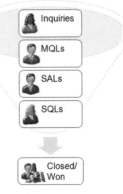

- **Marketing Qualified Lead (MQL)**—Using a broader set of carefully pre-defined criteria (ideally including a scoring algorithm agreed to by sales), marketing deems the

Figure 26: A framework for leads being handed from marketing to sales.

lead to be of sufficient quality to warrant sales engagement.

- **Sales Accepted Lead (SAL)**—Sales accepts the lead based on a preliminary review of the data on the lead, and agrees to engage with the prospect.

- **Sales Qualified Lead (SQL)**—Based on further conversations and interactions with the prospect, sales concurs that the lead is truly a revenue opportunity.

- **Closed Business**—Sales completes a transaction

Within this structure, a lead-scoring algorithm encapsulates the necessary criteria that are agreed to by both sales and marketing. From here, each group operates independently, either to drive the creation of MQLs (marketing) or to receive MQLs and drive toward revenue (sales). Synchronizing these metrics and aligning them around this structure creates a common language.

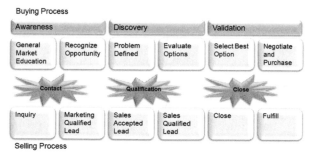

Figure 27: A lead-definition methodology that maps to the buyer's process.

☞ GET STARTED NOW

SALES ALERTS AND WEB SITE ACTIVITY

Even before you implement detailed lead-scoring algorithms and hand-off processes, you can give your sales team insights into their prospects. For instance, you can issue a real-time alert to a sales rep if a visitor reaches a threshold of Web site activity (such as a certain number of page views within a week, or a minimum number of site visits in a 30-day period). If the alert has detailed insights into the prospect's digital body language—what they looked at and what their relevant demographics are—the sales-person can use his own experience to determine his next steps and follow-up.

METRICS AND BEHAVIOR

In virtually every area of business, metrics drive behavior—especially when incentive-compensation elements are tied to those metrics. In marketing organizations, it's historically been a tricky task to define the right metrics, because the measurable elements of a marketing process (e.g. the raw number of inquiries) don't neatly align with actual business goals. That can lead to behaviors that are not optimal for the organization.

For instance, if the marketing organization is evaluated and compensated on the raw numbers of inquiries it generates, that organization almost inevitably will gravitate to activities (such as expensive give-aways and promotions) that yield large lists of raw names—*unqualified leads*—rather than devising and executing programs that help prospects move through a buying process.

⇨ *GET STARTED NOW*

GIVE SALES A THIRD WAY

Many times, leads are presented to sales too early in their buying process. That leaves only two options: sell hard and risk driving the prospect away or let the opportunity die. Neither is a defensible option. As a marketing team, you must provide sales with a third option—namely, an automated nurture campaign that retains the prospect until they are more ready. That keeps the communication channel open without selling too early or too aggressively.

Instead, we can align marketing activities with compensation incentives using digital body language to define the ideal marketing-qualified lead (MQL). That enables the marketing organization to create, track, and measure leads that are qualified and relevant to the goal of generating business for the organization. A marketing team that is measured and compensated based on the number of MQLs it generates will adopt longer-term perspectives and thoughtful campaigns and activities that create qualified leads that are acceptable to the sales team. What's more, a quota-driven sales team that's demanding a steady flow of MQLs will be well- motivated to ensure that the MQL definition is accurate and that the most relevant and important aspects of digital body language are well understood.

OBSERVATIONS VS. PROACTIVE MARKETING

Nonetheless, challenges can and do arise when marketers orient their efforts toward defined goals that are centered around scored leads based on digital body language. For example, an analysis of high-quality leads might reveal that, after a wide range of marketing activities and touchpoints, the crucial factors in determining quality were:

- The amount of time a prospect spends online

- The number of e-mails the prospect clicks on

- Whether the prospect visits a landing page

- Seeing a minimum of six pages of detailed solution information

From this information, the organization could build a lead-scoring algorithm to identify these leads and pass them to sales. However, the temptation arises to skew marketing efforts to simply focus solely on actions that are part of the scoring algorithm. As those marketing efforts shift to encourage the exact behavior measured by the scoring algorithm, the meaning and value of that behavior (in terms of qualification and sales readiness) decrease dramatically.

Let's use an extreme example to clarify the point. Suppose a marketing team wants to drive these behaviors outlined above because an analysis indicates that they correlate very highly with a qualified lead. The market-

⇨ *GET STARTED NOW*

GIVE SALES CONTENT THAT
LINKS TO THE WEB

Your sales team constantly communicates with prospects, whether it's an introduction, sending industry information such as case studies, or following up with a new white paper. For your marketing team to succeed in understanding buyers, it's essential to factor in this channel. Provide sales reps with electronic collateral in e-mail form with built-in tracking to the Web site so that each prospect is linked to his Web profile for visibility to their digital body language.

---

ing team might offer a free $100 gift card to the first 500 people who read six pages of solution information. While this would certainly drive the desired behavior, the lead-scoring algorithm that was correct before this campaign would no longer be accurate—the leads driven by the $100 offer would not be as sales-ready as previous leads were who read the six Web pages.

Lead-scoring algorithms are passive observations of historical buyer behavior. They are, most emphatically, *not* a set of predetermined steps to "create" a buyer. To reverse-engineer a lead-scoring algorithm to actively drive buyers is to once again slip into the outdated mentality of forcing a selling process rather than following a buying process.

To avoid this unintended consequence of adding metrics around scored leads, marketers can use MQL and SAL

⇨ *GET STARTED NOW*

DIGITAL BODY LANGUAGE IN CRM SYSTEMS
To ensure your sales team takes full advantage of the buyer's digital body language, you must present that information to them where they work— and typically that means CRM and e-mail systems. By using these applications to present a detailed view of an individual prospect's interests, what marketing they responded to, and what they searched for, your sales team can be more effective—without forcing them adopt a new technology.

statistics. By monitoring a MQL:SAL ratio, it's straightforward to see whether MQLs are spiking without a corresponding increase in SALs (indicating a corruption of the lead-scoring algorithm). This helps ensure that the motivation of the demand-generation team remains focused on creating leads that are accepted by the sales team.

One important challenge that must be addressed in building a coordinated sales and marketing organization is the existing systems of metrics. While metrics drive behavior, they can also create resistance to initiatives that change the group's ability to hit existing metric targets. If a metric that measures a particular group does not match with the overall transition, it may cause significant challenges in the overall process.

For example, a sales or telequalification group that is measured and compensated on the number of calls it makes each day will not quickly accept a business-process change that reduces the number of raw leads that are passed to it—regardless of the quality—because that reduction directly conflicts with how they are measured and reduces their compensation opportunity.

Executive sponsorship is therefore essential to ensuring that each group's metrics across the organization encourage rather than discourage the adoption of new marketing processes and approaches that leverage digital body language.

PROCESS CREATION AND BUY-IN

Cross-organizational departmental buy-in is equally necessary to ensure successful transitions to this new marketing paradigm. Since the laws of human nature haven't changed, the hesitation and uncertainty are only natural. Sales teams may resist new processes that mean fewer leads—even though the quality of those leads has risen dramatically and they have more high-quality opportunities to pursue.

Proof points can make the difference here. A well-structured process can achieve buy-in from sales quickly and effectively by demonstrating the greater effectiveness of digital body language throughout the sales cycle.

Clearly define the methodology for scoring leads and implement it in a manner that's hidden from sales. Continue to pass leads to sales without restrictions using the original process for an extended period of time—

⇨ *GET STARTED NOW*

PRESENTING THE DIGITAL
BODY LANGUAGE OF A COMPANY

Many sales teams work at the account level, not on an individual level. That means they are more interested in understanding what's happening in the aggregate at any given account. Roll up this information and present it to them in an aggregated lead score. Keep digital body language data at an individual level. In most cases, even a simple technique like a total sum of lead scores gives you a good indication of which companies are more interested.

---

perhaps 1-2x the average sales cycle length. Then, go back and correlate the score of the lead with the likelihood of that prospect closing, the size of the deal that eventually closes, or the speed with which it closes. That kind of data is immediately persuasive. Naturally, if no correlation is found, then the scoring algorithm is clearly flawed and must be refined.

The second advantage of this analysis is that it provides an understanding of where the bar should be set to pass a lead to sales vs. retaining it in the nurturing program.

Marketers can also secure stronger buy-in from sales when they provide clear visibility into the signs of digital body language in their raw form. If sales professionals see the digital body language characteristics for each of their prospects, and learn in real-time when certain online actions are taken or milestones are reached, it helps them understand the level of insight that marketing can now provide. As a result, sales is far more likely to be more engaged with the process of building a lead-qualification agreement using digital body language.

In demand-generation processes, the art of exception-handling is as important as the process itself. And with sales and marketing, the two most significant exceptions revolve around the clawback of leads not followed up on by sales and the cherry-picking by sales of leads that are not yet qualified.

CLAWBACKS

When a lead passes from marketing to sales—that is, after it meets the agreed lead-scoring threshold, it should be picked up by the appropriate salesperson and pursued. Of course, as any sales or marketing professional will candidly admit, this does not happen every time. These exceptions must be handled well, of course—but they also represent opportunities for learning and improvements. A lead that is not pursued by sales can be explicitly rejected, ignored, or picked up by a salesperson for whom it was not intended.

Each situation presents the chance to further optimize the lead-management process. If leads are explicitly rejected by sales, there is likely to be an opportunity to capture critical data on the rejection. *Why* was this lead rejected? Perhaps there are problems with the understanding of the prospects. Aggregated feedback from sales provides a strong basis for tightening the lead-scoring algorithm and ensuring a better alignment between the needs of sales and the qualities of the prospects.

It is a little more challenging in situations where leads are *not* being explicitly rejected. It may be that there is still a fundamental disconnect between sales and marketing—that sales does not fully believe the quality of the leads enough to pursue them. Of course, it's possible that sales is simply correct: the leads may, indeed, be poor. Regular calls between field marketing and sales enable quick identification of opportunities for improvement or areas where more data is required.

One tactic that is useful in some situations is to capitalize on the natural competitiveness among sales professionals. If a lead is not picked up and pursued by the assigned salesperson in a pre-determined period of time (e.g. one week), it can be automatically assigned to other appropriate salespeople. If the salesperson adopts the process and is rewarded with high-quality leads that have been passed over by other reps, he will begin to see the inherent value. The natural competitive dynamics of salespeople will factor into the process and the system will return to its balanced state.

Conversely, if there are an exceptional number of clawback leads, marketing and sales will need to jointly explore better methods of gaining acceptance of the process. This could involve marketing improving its presentation of the value of the information and scoring it provides.

CHERRY-PICKING

Marketing works with prospects to escort them through a sales process. Along the way, they achieve higher levels of qualification before they are handed off to sales. During that process, sales reps can usually identify high-potential leads—even though those leads are still early in the sales cycle—they aren't yet qualified. Given the revenue quota pressures they face, when they see contacts with the right roles and responsibilities at ideal target organizations, they often seek the ability to "cherry-pick" these best leads out of the process.

At first, that might seem like an excellent plan (especially when the entire organization faces quarterly revenue challenges), but it is imperative to resist this dangerous temptation. Remember, the new goal of contemporary marketing is to read the buyer's digital body language to understand his buying process and align your messaging with it. If the buyer's digital body language shows that this ideal executive at the ideal company is *not* ready to

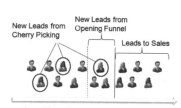

Qualification Level (scoring)

Figure 28: Allowing cherry-picking by sales results in less-qualified leads than a reduction in needed qualification level.

buy, then presenting an aggressive "salesy" message and attempting to prematurely engage a sales process can have the opposite desired effect: it can push the prospect away.

If the sales team is hungry for more leads, the answer isn't to cherry-pick leads that aren't nearly ready for sales engagement. The answer is to slightly loosen scoring criteria so that the greater volume of leads that do flow through to sales are the ones that are closest to MQL status—*not* simply the ones that look great at a quick glance based on title or company.

MARKETING ASSETS

What assets should marketing provide to the sales team—and how do they dovetail with the digital body language milestones and lead-scoring algorithm in place? Marketing communications efforts based on digital body language must leverage appropriate hooks and tracking codes to identify and understand the reactions of individual prospects. That's why it's critical for marketing to closely collaborate with sales to streamline the usage of marketing communications assets.

While a talented sales professional can craft a message that connects with a prospective buyer, it is extremely unlikely that he will build in the appropriate tracking mechanisms that identify the prospect's digital body language in any responses and incorporate that within the overall profile of that prospect. Marketing is on the hook for providing a 360-degree view of a prospect and is the only group with the breadth of communication and tracking tools to achieve this level of monitoring, data capture, interpretation, and escalation.

When we talk about tracking a marketing asset, most of us think of individual communication assets—such as e-mail or direct mail. But these are not the only types of asset that marketing can and should provide to sales. The extended, complex sales cycle also requires marketing to furnish sales with access to predefined communication programs for nurturing, establishment of thought leadership, introductions, or events. While a sales rep can often leverage his own intuition to assess where a prospect is in the buying process based on conversations, he doesn't have the capacity to continue to nurture and develop that prospect over time.

To optimize the sales/marketing collaboration, marketing must provide sales with sets of entry points where they can add prospects to specific nurturing, thought leadership, or invitation programs. If marketing provides these entry points to sales, marketing can take ownership of the prospect—with the appropriate monitoring and analysis of digital body language. Later, marketing can notify sales when that prospect shows the right digital body language (i.e. has become a MQL) and is ready for engagement with sales.

Sales reps, of course, want to track all of their leads—particularly monitoring for changes in status. Real-time alerts of significant actions and milestones allow sales to stay in tune with what's happening to prospects throughout their nurture cycle. This sales-marketing communication can help with achieving greater buy-in and comfort from sales, encouraging them to hand over their prospects to marketing with assurance that those leads aren't disappearing in a black hole.

When this level of coordination is achieved, sales clearly sees the benefits that marketing contributes in long-term prospect management. What's more, this exposure to the true lifecycle of a prospect encourages sales reps to gather and contribute more leads. Often, many organizations find that sales soon becomes a significant contributor of net new names, bringing an end to the "shadow marketing" that many sales reps undertake on their own.

Rather than waiting at a tradeshow for the perfect "ready-to-close" lead to show up at the booth, a sales team that has bought-in to marketing through digital body language voluntarily shifts toward collecting more contacts at *any* stage and enables marketing to nurture each of them until they are ready to engage more directly with sales.

THE SALES ENVIRONMENT

Coordination between marketing and sales requires more than providing the right value to sales people. It also means providing this value in the right, comfortable environment. As technology solutions continue to facilitate the necessary CRM processes, marketing technologies must conform to the way sales works in ways that facilitate adoption. Sales teams are, of course, notoriously slow to adopt new platforms, and are users of a limited number of technologies. That creates particular challenges for marketing, which must dovetail seamlessly into this world. The best way to proceed is for marketing to embed its tools and technologies within the technology that sales has already adopted.

In most organizations, this means the CRM system and client e-mail. Marketing has a better chance of succeeding by ensuring its assets and processes are accessible and available in one or both of these environments. In addition to assets, it will help to make the active profile information, scored leads, and buyer insight available in these environments as well.

This is a critical concern—and one that must be addressed upfront and immediately. Quite simply, without the information and the tools available to them in their preferred environments, the adoption rates will suffer greatly—and with it the value of digital body language approaches that marketing is pursuing.

ENDECA: SALES AND MARKETING RECONCILIATION

Endeca, a leader in Search and Information Access solutions, faced a challenge that confronts many marketing and sales teams. With a complex and sometimes lengthy sales cycle, it was difficult to measure the success of marketing campaigns and investments. Reporting on marketing's contributions to the bottom line was not well understood or measured and, as is the case with many marketing and sales teams, left the sales organization feeling disenchanted with marketing's ability to help drive revenue.

In an effort to generate and report on targeted leads, the marketing and sales teams forged agreement on the definition of a qualified lead. They also agreed to adopt a methodology of uploading and processing the leads and opportunities using an integrated Marketing Automation and CRM system. In addition, they scored the leads based on contact information and digital body language based on the goal of prioritizing people who had invested time and money learning about Endeca or their market. With marketing committed to delivering leads and sales committed to the follow up process, the executive team was now able to track significant progress on a dashboard reflecting the lead-to-deal funnel.

Marketing then adopted a "no secrets" policy to further strengthen relationships and credibility with the sales team. Every campaign was closely tracked and reports revealed exact investments as well as the resulting leads, opportunities, and pipeline value that was associated with each campaign. An internal newsletter, published calendar, real-time account activity notifications and live dashboards gave further company-wide visibility to these investments and successes.

The marketing team then made it a habit to familiarize themselves with campaigns that provided the highest yield of prospect meetings and largest closed deals. This practice gave them unique knowledge of how the company actually generated revenue, significantly increasing their credibility and value with the executive team.

With these initiatives in place, Endeca's marketing team is now able to better forecast the number of leads and opportunities required to support a specific industry, allowing them to create historical models of each conversion ratio and accurately predict the number of leads and opportunities required to achieve sales revenue targets. By strengthening the relationship between sales and marketing, from the executive suite to the field, Endeca's marketing team was able to become a key contributor to the overall pipeline.

INSIDE SALES, TELESALES, AND TELEQUALIFICATION

As they embrace the digital body language concept, marketing departments are working deeper into the funnel to nurture and qualify prospects. That leaves many organizations with a dilemma over how to structure the departments that loosely bridge the gap between marketing and sales—organizations like inside sales, telesales, telemarketing, telequalification, or demand generation. Fundamentally, these groups all perform one or two functions—tactical communication and deal making.

Tactical communication means making outbound calls to prospects at very specific stages in their buying process to deliver a targeted message, communicate a key idea, or generate an interim response such as event attendance. These communications are carefully crafted to align with other outbound communications, usually to carefully selected lists of prospects that have been segmented deliberately for this communication. The content in the message may be slightly personalized, but is relatively consistent. The response options to the message are likewise relatively limited: registering for an event, requesting further information, or handing-off to field sales.

With deal making, either inbound or outbound, the inside team is actually empowered to transact a deal and generate revenue. Usually, this model restricts the inside sales rep's target audience based on loose qualification status, deal size, product mix, or other metrics. These restrictions are much tighter than for a field team and, in most cases, face-to-face contact is limited or non-existent.

In thinking about the alignment and structure of tactical communications vs. deal-making, it is important to think of their roles. Many teams perform both roles in some proportion, but are more heavily weighted in one direction or the other. If the role is predominantly tactical communication, the ideal optimization is to use the timing and targeting of other communication tactics and measuring the response to determine whether the lead is qualified. This leads many organizations to

VMWARE: ALERTS TO ENABLE GLOBAL ACCOUNT TEAMS

The VMWare marketing team wanted to assist their Global Account Managers in their efforts to sell into a select list of targeted accounts. For the top 65 accounts, a high coverage model was in place with a Global Accounts Manager focused on only one or two accounts. To penetrate these accounts, the GAM would patiently work on areas of opportunities throughout the corporate hierarchy to maximize penetration.

To assist in this process, the VMWare marketing team created a weekly alert for each GAM on each global account that would summarize the activity across the entire account. Each contact that had shown interest or performed any action, from a two page web visit to a deep investigation of a new product, would be highlighted in the alert. The account rep would then have access to the full digital body language of each individual

As soon as it was rolled out across the team, this process began showing its success. Insights into activity would highlight teams in areas within an overall corporate structure that were, based on their actions, interested in virtualization solutions. By identifying these hot spots of activity, and identifying the exact product of interest for each hot spot, each GAM was able to identify individual buying processes that were happening at many levels in a global organization and sell accordingly.

The success of the initial rollout was such that the secondary tier of named accounts was added to the process, resulting in over 250 of VMWare's most focused sales reps having deep insight into the buying processes at their accounts of interest.

Synopsys: Centralized Marketing Communications

Synopsys is a world leader in software and IP for semiconductor design and manufacturing. As such, the sales process is very knowledge and education oriented. Sophisticated buyers and sophisticated sellers exchange lots of information throughout a lengthy process. Because of this, Synopsys discovered that each of their product marketing managers were sending micro campaigns to small lists of prospects at various stages of the education and sales process.

This had been a somewhat functional process, but did not allow Synopsys easy control of their brand and messaging and the risks of over-communicating to customers due to a lack of centralized control had become significant. It also did not allow Synopsys any insight into the digital body language of those prospects as each individual salesperson would send their small scale campaigns in their own way—often from their desktop—in a way that did not allow centralized tracking.

To operationalize these communications in a way that still allowed the knowledge-intensive sales process to progress, but gave Synopsys better control over brand and better ability to provide insights into their prospects' digital body language, they decided to centralize the process. Each salesperson could send any communication that they desired to, to any list of their prospects, but it would be executed centrally by a marketing service bureau (of one individual). This enabled consistency in brand messaging and started the process of keeping historical campaign data in one location.

As with any organization, there were pockets of resistance to either the creative standardization (all communications would now share a common look and feel) or to giving up control of a list of contacts. The centralization, however, offered three benefits that outweighed these hesitations. A common theme was more aesthetically pleasing than most of the individual efforts, winning over many. The reduction in effort was a second significant selling point. The ability to instantly see the results of each campaign, and the individuals who had clicked through and sought further information, was the final advantage to win over skeptics.

During two months, the transition was made to this new operational model. The field team was able to quickly craft the message and the target audience they had in mind, which was then passed to the central marketing service organization. By centralizing management of the final creative touches and the distribution of the messages, the marketing organization was able to maintain control over the branding and look and feel. The team was also able to ensure the proper tracking was in place to allow insight into the prospects' digital body language.

Through centralizing these communications, the Synopsys team was able to gain control over their brand and the frequency with which they communicate with prospects, while at the same time building rapport with their sales organization. By adding in the ability to observe the customers' digital body language, they also began to build a foundation for deeper insights into their audience, and for an internal culture of analytics.

conclude that these teams are most ideally allied with the marketing function that shares similar goals, tradeoffs, and outputs.

If the role is predominantly deal-making, the optimization takes place from the point at which a lead is qualified through to closing. The quality of leads passing into the group is a key driver—much as it is in sales. However, the qualities of sales technique differentiate the success of one individual in this group from another. For this reason, if the dominant role of the group is deal-making, most organizations will align that group with the sales team.

ALIGNMENT AND METRICS

Sales faces tremendous performance pressures because it's relatively straightforward to directly tie compensation to easily defined and measured performance metrics. As marketing begins to resolve age old alignment challenges with sales, this pressure will start to spill over into the marketing organization. To maintain credibility and guide strategic-investment choices in the end-to-end marketing and sales process, marketing needs a new approach to analytics.

NINE

CAN YOU FINALLY MEASURE MARKETING EFFECTIVENESS?

One of the persistent challenges in marketing: measuring and demonstrating its effectiveness in quantifiable ways. Although the value of marketing is generally accepted at a high level (few would accept the risks of under-investing in marketing, for instance), most business executives are unable to definitively articulate the precise contribution that marketing brings.

That becomes problematic in today's business climate, where the pressure for accountability increases public and investor scrutiny. Simultaneously, the rapid proliferation of new media in which to invest has marketers struggling to understand which options can deliver the greatest return.

In complex-sales environments, these pressures are magnified. Buying cycles can take months, encompass multiple communications vehicles and prospect touchpoints—all for a variety of prospects at various stages. Deciphering the effectiveness of a specific marketing initiative in such an environment is a daunting task.

The key is to approach the analysis challenge by first recognizing marketing's role in observing buyers' digital body language and accompanying prospects through their buying process by providing the right messages at the right times. Assessing the tactics that match prospects, timing, and messages, we gain a better understanding of how to allocate resources across media types to optimize ROI.

THE LEAD-SOURCE PARADOX

Many analysts start off by focusing on the concept of "lead source." When a deal closes, the analyst credits the marketing initiative that originally surfaced that prospect, and an analysis framework is built around that structure. Unfortunately, this methodology does not yield high-value insights or an accurate picture of the marketing landscape in anything but the simplest of B2B sales environments.

That's because, as we have seen, the prospective buyer is not suddenly "driven" to make a purchase because of a well-crafted marketing campaign or elegantly worded collateral documents. Rather, a purchase is the culmination of a well-choreographed series of messaging, campaigns, and collateral that—over time—*collectively* guide the prospective buyer through education and discovery processes that are driven by their own internal

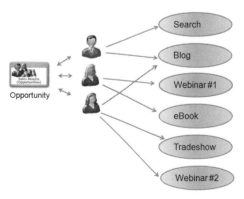

Figure 29: The lead source paradox: each opportunity is influenced in many ways.

interests and business goals. Somewhat randomly choosing the last message, document, event, or campaign and proclaiming that it is the sole driver of the purchase is a deeply flawed structure for analysis that can lead to ill-informed and unfortunate decisions regarding subsequent marketing investments.

That complexity grows exponentially when one acknowledges that there is not just one individual making a purchase decision. Teams of influencers, evaluators, and decision makers are receiving these messages, documents, and campaigns. A high-performing and successful marketing organization influences all of these individuals—whether it's guiding them to recommend a solution, inspire them to push for it, motivate them to approve it, or convince them not to object to it.

This prospect communication begins long before the active selling process initiates. It may reflect months or years of steady, persistent, and artful nurturing before a buying event in the prospect's organization drives them to engage more actively. Marketing communications also continue during the active phase of the buying process. To attempt to simplify this buying environment down to a single "lead source" is attempting to simplify more than the realities of the situation can logically support.

MARKETING INVESTMENT ALLOCATION

Once marketers can analyze and better understand the impact of their marketing initiatives on prospective buyers, they are in a good position to make smarter decisions on how to optimally allocate their investments to have the greatest positive effects on revenue. By returning to the stages of the buying process, and mapping these to relevant metrics, marketers gain an understanding of what phases in the buying-process funnel require more effort.

Initiatives to generate awareness may be measured in terms of traffic or raw inquiries. Marketing campaigns aiming to connect with buyers at the solution-discovery stage may generate inquiries driven by searches or inquiries on certain marketing assets such as downloadable demos. Programs to connect to buyers at the solution-validation stage or guide them into this stage may generate MQLs that are passed to sales.

By recognizing what stages buyers are at and properly allocating marketing investments, marketers can enhance their ability to guide prospects to the next stage of the buying process. Achieving this while ensuring coordinated hand-offs to sales, marketing generates a comprehensive picture of its investments.

Understanding the influence of campaigns on buyers at various stages of the process and using digital body language to assess campaign results, marketers may finally achieve a more complete picture of marketing ROI.

Marketing ROI

Assessing the ROI for marketing initiatives and campaigns must start with a sound understanding of the realities of the complex buying cycle. For instance, a marketing budget may allocate significant dollars to identifying prospects who are in the early stages of their awareness or discovery cycle. While the value of these efforts to the overall marketing strategy isn't open to question, their direct impact will not necessarily show up in the spreadsheet because the prospects they reach are so early in the purchasing cycle. Other activities and touchpoints will subsequently take place before the leads are passed to sales.

If we agree that today's marketing revolves around steering a buyer through an entire ecosystem by delivering the right messages to the right people at the right time, then the only effective and proper way to measure a marketing ROI is to assess it in the aggregate. The metric that matters is high level: the ability of the company's overall marketing investments to drive the output of qualified leads. More granular analysis should only compare the individual initiative or campaign against its intended effects.

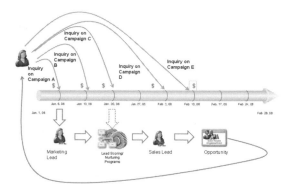

Figure 30: Influence and attribution of marketing campaigns

In fact, the larger challenge in measuring a marketing ROI lies in quantifying the output. Since marketing's contribution creates a qualified lead, which itself has only a given possibility (not statistical certainty) of closing, the question becomes: how do we quantify that output to calculate an ROI?

Ideally, we'd like to directly connect marketing investments straight through to the profits derived from the corresponding revenue events that result. Unfortunately, of course, the world isn't anywhere near that cut-and-dried. There are too many intervening profitability variables (e.g. sales effectiveness) that complicate the analysis.

The simplest way to measure marketing's contribution is to measure it through to a marketing-qualified lead and/or sales-accepted lead. This still leaves room for an analysis that carries through to revenue, but that is a layer that should remain secondary to MQL or SAL analysis because it introduces too many other contributing factors that lie outside the scope of marketing effectiveness.

INFLUENCE AND ATTRIBUTION: THE NEW MEASUREMENT STRUCTURE

To account for the complexities of analyzing the complex-sales process, we need a new analysis framework. Every marketing campaign must have a clear overarching goal. It could be to educate prospects, remain top-of-mind, establish a structure for competitive comparison, or encourage prospects to begin their engagement with the sales team. Tracking a prospect's digital body language gives us a way to understand whether this campaign influenced the prospect in the right way—that influence is what we want to focus on.

However, each campaign derives its influence in varying ways. We can judge a campaign that targets nurturing prospects as a successful influence simply if the recipient reads the message without taking any action. A different campaign, however, might require a prospect to act (e.g. visit a personalized URL or click on a link) before we can conclude that it influenced the prospect. Or—building the intensity of interaction—a different campaign might drive prospects to take more explicit action such as submitting a form or downloading a white paper. Influence for these latter campaigns is measured by whether the recipient prospect took these affirmative actions.

Given the breadth of campaigns that marketers execute in most complex-purchase environments, analysts will often find that *many* campaigns exert influence over the creation of a revenue opportunity. Attempting to deduce which campaign deserves the "credit" for a single lead is highly inexact and prone to mistaken assumptions. Instead, the analyst should assign a percentage of the revenue opportunity to each relevant campaign that influenced the prospect. The model can be defined and continually adjusted by the organization. The campaigns that build the value proposition prior to sales' direct engagement can be assigned a certain percentage of the value. Campaigns that capture direct buyer interest receive a separate percentage of the value and campaigns that initially connect a named buyer at the organization with a sales engagement receive another percentage of the total value.

Once marketing has crafted a model to calculate the influence of campaigns on prospect behavior and modeled how the influencing campaigns should be attributed to the appropriate amount of revenue from opportunities, it's a relatively simple matter to understand the effects of marketing campaigns. However, building this analysis framework requires analysts to assess tactics, initiatives, and campaigns.

⇨ *GET STARTED NOW*

A DISCIPLINE OF ANALYSIS: SEARCH

Many marketing organizations lack the ability to systematically analyze data because, traditionally, they have dealt with very untrackable media types. Start to create a culture of analysis by looking at each tactic's performance. Look at search results on a weekly basis to understand what people are looking for when they find you. Which searches indicate market education, vendor discovery, or solution comparison? Which searches lead to viewing or downloading marketing assets? Do those search queries yield the right assets based on their buying cycle? Through careful search analysis, you can develop both a deeper understanding of your buyers and a baseline for future comparison.

MEASURING MARKETING TACTICS

Marketing analysts should start with an assessment of marketing tactics and the responses that these tactics elicit from prospects. Each tactic—a direct-mail drop, marketing e-mail message, landing page, search campaign, Web form, white paper, or Flash demo—must be considered in terms of its own singular inherent goal as well as for the digital body language signs it spurs if the prospect responds. The analysis should also consider how the digital body language provides insights into other areas or interests.

If the tactic is driving attendance to an event, it will be structured and analyzed quite differently than a tactic that nurtures prospects. Next, we should analyze the actions that are available to prospects—based on their meaning in terms of digital body language—and determine three metrics: tracking of action, depth of interest measured, and breadth of interest measured.

- **Tracking of Actions**—Most new media can be monitored down to the individual recipient level. For instance, most contemporary e-mail systems let marketers track who opened the e-mail to read and who subsequently clicked through links in the e-mail. Personal URLs (www.mycampaign.com/JohnSmith) are ideal vehicles with direct mail pieces because they enable marketers to present uniquely personalized response messages to each recipient while allowing the marketer to understand the responses. Search campaigns can be tracked down to the keyword and ad copy, and can help marketers better understand the intentions and goals of each prospect.

- **Depth of Interest**—This metric provides much greater levels of insight into prospects' true intentions and motivations. It's the difference between a prospect who sees something in a marketing message that catches his eye, prompting a quick one-page visit, and a prospect who read the same interesting message but spent more than 15 minutes at the site, reviewing 12 pages. Likewise, we can assess depth of interest by observing whether the prospect progresses to the next action. Analyzing an e-mail campaign to understand who opened it is a good first step. But it is identifying the prospects who clicked on links, visited the landing page, viewed other pages, and submitted Web forms that provides the marketer with much more insight about that buyer's depth of interest. Today's marketers must analyze tactics at this level to understand how effective they are in engaging the digital buyer.

- **Breadth of Interest**—Similarly, a sound marketing analysis focuses on the breadth of interest shown by the prospect. Each interaction and prospect touchpoint provides marketers with an opportunity to refine their understanding of areas their prospects are most interested in. It's important, therefore, to configure each tactic to capture this data. Marketers should ensure they understand whether a specific marketing tactic drove interest in certain product lines or service offerings. We also need to know whether the prospect was more engaged by the offer of the free giveaway than by thought leadership white papers that were also included in the offer and whether the main content or the secondary feed of related articles in a sidebar was the main driver of prospect click-through.

Only with this clear understanding of each tactic's performance can we begin to analyze the performance of

NetQoS: Analyzing Viral Campaigns

As discussed earlier, NetQoS ran a highly successful viral-video marketing campaign. But the big challenge for any marketer executing a viral campaign is to quantify its success. A focus on analytics was built into the fabric of the viral marketing effort for NetQoS and helped document its success.

First, everything was trackable: Web pages, video views, requests, blogs, and more. A viral campaign breaks big and fast, leaving no time for testing - so there's no substitute for thoughtful tracking and analysis strategies. For example, NetQoS analyzed aggregate and individual-visitor analytics to understand exactly how viewers made their way to product pages and trial downloads.

Since it was an awareness-based campaign, before/after metrics were compared on Google search-term exposure, showing a 41 percent increase in search-term exposure across all NetQoS keywords and a 600 percent increase on the most specific terms. Blog exposures and mentions were tracked carefully as well. The viral campaign led to coverage on more than 70 blogs, driving awareness of NetQoS throughout the market.

For leads explicitly driven to download a trial, a source code was captured to mark that as viral, enabling NetQoS to confidently credit the campaign with a 400 percent increase in trial registrants in the month the campaign launched. Since these leads led to meetings, the initial source (the viral campaign) was carried forward as a credited source for the meetings.

Although the viral campaign was the fifth-highest source for driving meetings in 2007, it ranked second on opportunity value per meeting showing that it achieved an excellent connection with the right audience for NetQoS products.

overall marketing initiatives in a manner that accurately reflects their contribution to the organization.

MEASURING MARKETING INITIATIVES

Of course, successful marketing communications in the complex-sales environment isn't driven by one-time standalone tactical communications—these are only the building blocks of larger strategic marketing initiatives. These might include event campaigns (webinars, tradeshows, or multi-city tours) promotional campaigns (product launches, price discounts, or customer success announcements). They might also encompass higher-level strategic campaigns such as entry into a new vertical market or geography, or a focused effort on a specific market segment such as small and medium businesses or enterprise-class organizations. For each of these initiatives, marketers deploy a *series* of tactical communications to facilitate an outcome.

To analyze these initiatives, we must first understand the outcomes being sought. Is it an attempt to raise awareness in a given industry? Perhaps it's an initiative to establish the parameters by which competitors are compared. It could be a pre-emptive effort to diffuse potential objections. The campaign could also be an attempt to encourage potential champions to actively engage in a buying process. Regardless of the goal, each initiative must be measured accordingly using distinct and carefully calibrated measurement approaches.

It's helpful to view and analyze each marketing initiative as guiding and accompanying buyers as they move from one stage in the buying process to the next. If the goal of an initiative is to create more awareness in the pharmaceutical sector on the East Coast of the U.S., then the key success metric to measure is the number of prospects at the awareness/discovery phase that have been influenced by the initiative. If the goal is to spur prospects to engage with sales, the key success metric is the number of MQLs that were directly influenced and motivated by that campaign.

Of course, as we know, prospects are not necessarily driven by marketing messages, but by their own internal business needs. Every marketing initiative can highlight the easiest path to the next phase, present compelling motivations to take that path, and clarify the benefits of doing so. But unless there is a current and compelling internal business need at the prospect's organization, even the highest-quality marketing initiative will likely be very ineffective. What's more, unless the prospect is sufficiently far along in his understanding of the market and available solutions, it is unlikely that he will be ready to move forward a step.

Even if the prospect does express an interest in engaging with the sales organization prior to developing a solid understanding of the market, it is still quite possible— even likely—that he is interacting with sales prematurely—which only wastes the time of the sales team. These prospects are the "tire kickers" who request information,

SYBASE: PROCESS AND ANALYSIS ECOSYSTEM

As a billion-dollar enterprise software company, Sybase has a broad and complex sales and marketing ecosystem. For the Sybase marketing team, given that they are a provider of some of the industry's leading database and analytics products, and have highly analytical executives, this leads to a need to present a clear overview of what is happening within marketing to all levels of the organization.

To do this, the Sybase team focused on three key areas of analytics; sales effectiveness, campaign success, and coverage optimization. The first of these analytics efforts, sales effectiveness, became the focus of the bi-weekly pipeline review between sales and field marketing. For each region, a detailed review of marketing activity and prospect response would be performed for the key accounts in the region. Highlights of the prospects' digital body language in accounts that had gone quiet would be used to trigger different account strategies for those accounts.

The second focus, campaign success, was a marketing-driven effort to analyze the effectiveness of campaigns against stated goals. Each campaign would be given different goals based on the call to action (ie, web seminar marketing campaigns would be analyzed on % registered whereas telemarketing campaigns would be analyzed on qualified leads captured). The campaigns were then analyzed against expected goals to understand where successes were being achieved and where ideas could be better shared. This analysis generally remained at the tactical level, as, given the length of the buying process in question, the macro analysis found marketing influence in over 90% of deals.

The third main focus, coverage optimization, was again done as a bi-weekly exercise. Top level marketing expenditure amounts were defined based on industry comparables, but within that overall framework, each expense item was coded by region and product. Comparing both marketing expenditures and prospect interest levels on a region and product grid allowed Sybase to identify areas in need of additional focus and reallocate investments quickly to the needed regions.

By leveraging its own analytics technology to better understand the digital body language of its prospects, Sybase was able to provide its sales team, its marketing team, and its executive team with a previously unavailable understanding of what was and was not working in the revenue funnel.

demos, and conversations, but are not ready to make a decision. Any analysis of marketing initiatives must use metrics that reflect this reality.

By setting the parameters of marketing goals up front—the conversion of prospects from one phase of their buying process to the next—the marketing team can both target the right set of prospects (in the target phase of their buying process) and the right set of messaging (to drive prospects to the next appropriate phase).

MEASURING RETURN

Building on this foundation of analysis of both tactics and initiatives, marketers now have the ability to understand the return they are achieving on their marketing investments. As we've seen, various initiatives can be relevant at all stages of the sales process. However, depending on the stage, they may not tie directly to the

COGNOS: MARKETING ANALYTICS OF A BI LEADER

Cognos, IBM's business intelligence and performance management subsidiary, needed stronger alignment between sales and marketing. With a high-value product and a complex sales cycle that often extended more than 9 months, however, this was a complicated proposition.

Many campaigns influence a Cognos buyer over a long period of time, so it was difficult to show marketing's precise influence on new and existing pipeline opportunities. It was also difficult to see the number and age profile of opportunities that had passed from marketing to sales. Without these key performance indicators, sales/marketing alignment was elusive at best.

Cognos's own business intelligence products gave it a distinct advantage. By pulling deep, detailed metrics on marketing activities and comparing these to the pipeline, marketing created dashboards on marketing influence. The most successful was a dashboard showing marketing activities for accounts owned by a particular individual. This provided each salesperson with a clear view as to the type and amount of marketing activity that was influencing his accounts and strengthened his understanding of exactly what marketing was doing to help him succeed.

One sales cycle clearly showed the value of this approach, when an opportunity seemed to be progressing well, until it suddenly went silent. Reviewing this dashboard, the sales rep noticed that 67 activities had happened in the past 2 weeks. No longer did the opportunity appear dead, but instead it was clear that Cognos was still very much in the game.

Combined with dashboards of metrics on marketing contribution to pipeline, and age profiles on sourced opportunities, this metric-oriented approach to marketing enabled sales and marketing to better align their objectives. Bi-weekly interlock calls between marketing and sales run in all regions where a regional marketing member works with the sales team to better understand current sales activities, marketing activities across the region, and response profiles within the top 10 deals. Sales, in turn, has accountability for follow-up with all marketing-sourced opportunities within 30 days.

While assisting the sales team on a region-by-region basis, the Cognos marketing team is also developing a deeper understanding of what an active buyer looks like. By performing a recency/frequency/role analysis across their marketing base, Cognos began to see that the time between interactions was a key indicator of peak interest. If the time between interactions went above 10 days, the chance of their being an active buying interest dropped dramatically.

Using these insights, the Cognos team catered their offer sequence to prospects based on the typical engagement path for interested buyers. Unique paths of offers, emails, and web content were crafted for each interest profile. By doing this, the marketing team was able to increase open rates by nearly 2X and increase clickthrough rates over 8X, showing a significant uplift in prospect engagement.

leads that are handed over to sales. To understand the marketing ROI, marketers must view these initiatives as a *portfolio* of investments that, collectively, generate desired outcomes.

The premise is that each tactic in each campaign that connects with a prospective buyer influences that buyer's purchase decision in one form or another. Marketers must monitor and measure the influence of these tactics across a portfolio of initiatives. As these initiatives nurture, engage, remove objections, and build relationships with prospects, many prospects will move down the funnel toward a sales engagement. As they move down the funnel, marketers select and use different, carefully calibrated campaigns to influence and engage with them. By the time a revenue event happens, the prospect has been exposed to a broad set of influences resulting from various marketing initiatives.

To build an aggregate profile of the influence of the entire portfolio of initiatives, marketers must apply the same discipline they used to analyze individual tactics and initiatives. By drawing together a rich profile of this portfolio, marketers can link back each opportunity or closed deal to the set of initiatives that favorably influenced it.

Once the marketer establishes the set of initiatives that influenced the revenue event, the next step is to allocate that revenue across those campaigns. This can be modeled in a manner appropriate to the length of sales process and areas that are judged to be the most challenging.

The first campaign to initiate a dialogue and establish a relationship with a prospect receives a certain percentage of the revenue. The campaign that persuades the prospect to engage with the sales professional is attributed another percentage of the revenue. In this way, a model can be established and optimized to allocate appropriate amounts of revenue to each campaign in the portfolio.

THE MEASURED MARKETING ORGANIZATION

Each stage in the funnel is uniquely valuable, and each transition between stages is uniquely challenging. Collectively, they enable the buyer to become aware of a solution area, understand the available options, decide that he sees a need for that solution, evaluate potential options, select a vendor, and close a deal.

That implies a daunting series of transitions that the buyer must proceed through. The organization that provides the right information to that buyer based on the stage he is at and the level of interest he demonstrates is most likely to succeed. To help ensure this success, marketing must understand which prospects are at what stages, what thought processes they go through as they move from stage to stage, and how to optimally provide the information they need to make those transitions.

Without a constant and clear recognition of this buying process, marketing analysis can easily drift to focus on the wrong set of measurements.

1 0 TEN

THE FUTURE
OF MARKETING

In the past decade, marketing has witnessed an unprecedented proliferation of ways to access a rapidly broadening array of resources. Most profoundly, this overarching trend has reshaped how buyers discover, analyze, understand, compare, and purchase products in complex sales cycles. While marketing (and sales) have begun to successfully adopt these technologies to communicate with prospects, they've only recently begun to incorporate this transformation into their strategies to effectively influence the new digital buyer.

But it's happening. Marketing now understands—more than ever—that it must collect a broader range of information on the prospect's role, areas of interest, and intensity of interest. Marketing now understands that it must bring together these disparate data points to create a unified, coherent, and comprehensive profile of the buyer.

As this understanding grows, marketers are taking greater advantage of the capabilities that new media types afford: search, e-mail, and variable-data printing—to provide personalized and customized communications that reflect each buyer's unique situation and goals. The ability to understand what prospects do and what they are interested in grows ever more crucial—more so than mere title or size of the buying organization. As a result, marketers are seeking more and newer ways to more deeply understand what their prospects truly want and execute creative campaigns that capitalize on these insights into motivations (instead of yesterday's "creativity for creativity's sake" mentality).

Borrowing from peers in financial services who use similar methodologies for credit rankings, marketers have adapted techniques to score leads and gain a more sound, more nuanced perspective on their prospects' propensities to take desired actions. As marketers continue to refine the combined art/science of translating digital body language into actionable insights, new thinking and new techniques for engaging with prospects are emerging.

CHANGES IN STAFFING

This transition is propelling the growth of the analytical marketer—the individual who most often enters the marketing field from disciplines that are traditionally strong in operational thinking, such as supply-chain management, finance, and IT. Marketers are beginning to capture, store, and process unprecedented volumes of data and will also need people with management capabilities and skills to model, prototype, and design processes. Already, our industry is seeing job postings for this role that indicate a growing demand that outstrips supply.

This transition in the type of individual entering the marketing profession has far-reaching implications. Marketing instruction must adapt to the challenges of the contemporary practice of marketing. Current curricula focus on either the creative challenges of marketing or the brand challenges of consumer marketing (with classic frameworks such as the "Four Ps"). However, the challenges facing tomorrow's marketers will require new skill sets not found in the syllabi at today's leading marketing schools.

As this transformation accelerates and marketing departments necessarily become metric-focused, disciplined operational groups, compensation plans must also evolve. While departments focused on creative disciplines can be notoriously difficult to evaluate, departments focused on measurable, objective goals are not. With metrics come both accountability and proof of results. However, with proof of results comes the demand for commensurate compensation. In much the same way that the compensation for top sales professionals can outpace their lower performing colleagues by factors of even five or more, we may see marketing compensation schemes align themselves more directly with performance as objective metrics make this viable.

EXECUTIVE ALIGNMENT

In parallel, the relationship between marketing and sales will continue to evolve as well. The common currency of the scored lead now permits marketing and sales to speak a common language and coordinate hand-off points that are jointly defined. As a result, the ability to optimize the end-to-end process increases. As this ability to coordinate and optimize grows, the two disciplines will begin to converge and, with that, the need will grow for executives who understand both sales and marketing as constituent parts of a new and broader revenue-generation process.

As sales and marketing optimize their processes to span both departments, they will also gain a greatly enhanced ability to analyze successes and challenges across the full spectrum of the sales cycle. These new-breed analytics will create a much clearer ability to understand both the value of sales and marketing investments, and the optimal inflection points that merit greater investment allocations. This, in combination with the more operational disciplines in marketing, will drive both the opportunity and the need for more understanding of marketing's inner workings from a financial perspective.

This transition, paired with the many changes underway within marketing itself, may lead to a fundamental shift in the alignment of the sales and marketing groups themselves. Once the end-to-end process of creating revenue is understood and optimized—from demand generation through sales—it may make more sense to assign overall authority to a single executive leader, rather than separate heads of sales and marketing reporting into a CEO.

Regardless of whether that specific executive shift itself takes place, marketing's transition to an accountable discipline will likely lead to a significant positive shift in the boardroom relationship between marketing and the executive team. Through the ability to demonstrate its results, marketing develops the credibility to ask for more budget. That brings an increase in the clout of the marketing leader, and perhaps a corresponding increase in the longevity of marketing leadership within an organization.

WEB 2.0 AND THE ONGOING EVOLUTION OF MARKETING

As Web 2.0 and social computing continue to rapidly evolve, marketing will continue to witness this profound change in the way in which prospects gather and evaluate information. Instead of static communication from vendors, analysts, and the media, prospects will increasingly turn to dynamic, peer-sourced information. Currently, much of this information resides in recorded forms (blogs, tagging, commentaries). However, it's likely that it will evolve to even more dynamic forms as buyers connect with colleagues in real time for trusted recommendations.

The simplicity of creating and sharing richer content such as video, audio, and animation is also having a profound and far-reaching effect on marketing. Experiences can be captured and shared in ways that are far more impactful than words and pictures. The influence of these new media types is likely to grow as prospective buyers continually seek to better understand the market they are in and the solutions that are available.

Each of these evolutions will challenge marketers to reevaluate the ways they engage with and understand their prospects. Although tactics will naturally shift and evolve, the fundamental principle will remain unchanged: marketers must identify and leverage digital body language to better engage with buyers. Success will accrue to marketers who are best able to see each new evolution as an opportunity to optimize their delivery of the right message to the right person at the right time.

The wealth of granular, timely data these vehicles can produce will also allow marketers new ways to understand, and ideally influence, the perceptions of their brand in the market. In the social media sphere, marketers can use the tenets of digital body language to understand how, when, and why individuals are interacting with the brand, and whether that impression is positive or negative. That will help them tailor their messaging and fine-tune their ability to influence this brand perception. The association of a product with a category, the reshaping of how solutions in a category are evaluated, or the perception of a product within that category are all brand-related challenges that tomorrow's marketers must tackle using digital body language principles.

Data Access

As this new paradigm for marketing evolves, market-ers must continue to carefully consider the continually evolving ability to access data on companies and con-tacts. Historically, the data itself was an inherent asset. It was bought and sold at significant prices. However, the basic assumptions relating to data are rapidly changing. The advent of a variety of new data sources and social networks, combined with the fact that data itself can be copied infinitely, has caused the value of data itself to drop continuously. The value of the relationship, how-ever, is enormous.

With a near-universal access to data through a variety of means and in a variety of forms, it's quite likely that we will see an evolution in approaches to managing rela-tionships and permissions. Many of today's headlines fo-cus on the regulatory aspects of this permission, and this is a key element, but as technology increasingly enables prospects to disconnect from unwanted messaging, the spirit of the law is what becomes more critical.

Of course, regardless of how ethically and scrupulously the marketer acquires and manages its data, if the recipi-ent is no longer engaged with the messaging, the rela-tionship is over. Marketers must manage and understand permission to engage in a dialogue from the perspective of the recipient, not from the perspective of a legal or policy directive.

Savvy marketers recognize this and are building their processes to manage and strengthen trusted relationships with their prospects. That trust builds from the marketer's understanding the prospects digital body language. The signs will continue to evolve and enhance these processes as data becomes increasingly available. Marketers who fail to adopt this new paradigm will see deteriorating results as recipients tune out their messaging either by blocking it or by ignoring it.

PROCESS EVOLUTION

As communication media types and data access evolve, so, too, will the various marketing processes discussed in this book. The advent of technologies such as Web services and software as a service (SaaS) show us that it is continually becoming easier to integrate previously disparate aspects of the business. Point-of-sale systems, transaction systems, shipping systems, or other relevant systems within the organization are adopting Web services and integrating within a technology framework. And that gives marketers new opportunities to blend those disciplines and services into a broader view of the marketing challenge and solution.

The same philosophy—understanding the prospect and delivering the right message to the right person at the right time—will continue to guide forward-thinking marketing teams. But with richer and deeper sources of information to integrate into the new fabric of marketing, it becomes increasingly easier to create richer, more comprehensive views of each prospect. Similar philosophies will evolve around understanding the motivations of existing customers and using that understanding to deliver up-sell, cross-sell, renewal, and retention messaging.

Many contact centers have begun to explore this evolving integration of customer behavior data (e.g., connection with a contact center) with explicit customer data (e.g., data on customer purchase history or lifetime value) to guide interactions. As the discipline evolves, marketers will continue to seek a broader lens with which to understand their customers and prospects. That broader lens will lead them to engage with sources of information throughout the enterprise to build a richer picture of prospects and their propensity to purchase.

THE MARKETING VALUE CHAIN

As marketers increasingly gain the ability to assess the value of various prospect actions, it's likely that the overall marketing value chain may find ways to improve its business models. In a manner similar to the evolution from cost-per-impression advertising to cost-per-click, marketers may find themselves restructuring their value chain and compensating partners and agencies on a performance basis. For instance, the value of a campaign that generates given numbers of a certain type of prospect can be clearly understood and valued.

A similar logic applies to prospects themselves. A deeper understanding of the value of each stage allows marketers to pinpoint the equitable exchanges of value that makes sense at each stage. However, this is less likely to evolve as much because of the inherent propensity of the system to self-adjust. Less-interested prospects can skew the system because a more generous offer draws in more people with less interest in the underlying product.

The role of today's marketer retains many aspects of its creative heritage. However, the challenge becomes understanding the motivations and emotions of prospective—but faceless—buyers at each individual stage of the buying process. By understanding who these prospects are and targeting them with the right message at the right time to elicit the exact emotional response needed, marketing can facilitate the buying process in new ways. The *who* and *when* of messaging, as we've seen, is guided by an understanding of the buyers' digital body language. The content, however, is still an art form that gives a great marketer the latitude to achieve what a less talented marketer never could.

AN EXCITING ERA

There's never been a more exciting time to be a marketer. With new ways of connecting with prospects and understanding their needs, a growing number of marketing organizations are embarking on a journey to leverage the new insights in ways that were unimaginable even 10-15 years ago.

Each technology that is adopted on a wide scale will significantly impact how, when, and what information is exchanged. As marketers, we must continually put ourselves in the shoes of our prospects and persevere in our efforts to understand how that transition in acquiring information may mean a transition in the way that we communicate.

At each step, marketers must also seek to understand how we can use that interesting and previously unknown information to better understand our prospects, refine our marketing initiatives, and better serve the needs of our target markets and sales and marketing organizations.